MW01054867

VULTURE
in a CAGE

Poems by

Solomon Ibn Gabirol

translated and introduced by

Raymond P. Scheindlin

archipelago books

The Hebrew text of Ibn Gabirol's secular poems is taken from *Shelomo ibn gabirol: shirei
haḥol,* edited by Ḥayim Brody and Ḥayim Schirmann, published by the Schocken Institute
of the Jewish Theological Seminary of America (1974).

The devotional poems are drawn from Dov Jarden, *Shirei haqodesh lerabi shelomo ibn gabirol*
(1971–73). The first volume was privately published. The second was published under the
auspices of the American Academy for Jewish Research.

Archipelago Books
232 3rd Street #A111
Brooklyn, NY 11215
www.archipelagobooks.org

Library of Congress Cataloging-in-Publication Data
Names: Ibn Gabirol, active 11th century, author. | Scheindlin, Raymond P.,
translator.
Title: Vulture in a cage : poems by Solomon Ibn Gabirol / translated by
Raymond P. Scheindlin.
Description: First Archipelago Books edition. | Brooklyn, NY : Archipelago,
2016. | A selection of Gabirol's poems never before published together as
a collection.
Identifiers: LCCN 2016027341 (print) | LCCN 2016033773 (ebook) | ISBN
9780914671558 (paperback) | ISBN 9780914671565 ()
Subjects: LCSH: Ibn Gabirol, active 11th century--Translations into English.
| Hebrew poetry. | BISAC: POETRY / Ancient, Classical & Medieval. | POETRY
/ Inspirational & Religious.
Classification: LCC PJ5050.I3 A2 2016 (print) | LCC PJ5050.I3 (ebook) | DDC
892.41/2--dc23
LC record available at https://lccn.loc.gov/2016027341

Distributed by Penguin Random House

Cover art: Danielle English
www.Kanizo.co.uk

Composition: Miles B. Cohen

Archipelago Books gratefully acknowledges the generous support from the National
Endowment for the Arts, the New York State Council of the Arts (a state agency), and the
New York City Department of Cultural Affairs.

PRINTED IN THE UNITED STATES OF AMERICA

TO

Ezekiel Alexander Scheindlin

AND

Lila Ayelet Scheindlin

CONTENTS

ACKNOWLEDGMENTS

Thanks are due to my former student Dr. Michael Rand, for providing information from the database of the Academy of the Hebrew Language on manuscripts containing poems by Ibn Gabirol; to my friend Professor Stephen Geller, for his invaluable early critique of the translations; to my friends Professors Mark Cohen and Walter Blanco for their critical reading of the introduction; and, especially, to my wife, Janice Meyerson, who directed her fierce drive for accuracy and good taste at the manuscript of this book, as she has with my previous writings, and indeed, at everything she undertakes. She earns a special tip of the hat for contributing one word, but a powerful one, to the translation of one of the poems. Thanks to Hebrew typographer Miles Cohen and his sharp grammarian's eye for the pains he took with the vocalized Hebrew text. The Hebrew typesetting was made possible by a generous grant from the Shalom Spiegel Institute of Medieval Hebrew Poetry of the Jewish Theological Seminary of America. I am grateful to Jill Schoolman of Archipelago Books for taking this book under her wing and championing the poetry of Solomon Ibn Gabirol.

My translations of a few of the poems have appeared in earlier publications. For the purposes of this book, these translations have been thoroughly revised or completely redone.

INTRODUCTION

Just see your servant's suffering and misery.
Just see his soul, a vulture in a trap.

Ibn Gabirol in His World

The image of himself as a violent creature furious at being trapped and frantic at being unable to fulfill his natural desire to soar free marks Ibn Gabirol as a singular voice among the poets of the Hebrew Golden Age. Two generations after his death, he was still remembered as an angry man. Yet the poetics of the age did not favor extreme expressions of violent emotion. Ibn Gabirol's poetic peers were accustomed to presenting strongly held ideas and deeply felt emotions in a literary style and in poetic forms that depend on and evoke harmony and balance.

We know very little about what made Ibn Gabirol such an extreme figure; in fact, what we do know about him boils down to very little. He is believed to have been born around 1021 in Málaga and to have died in Valencia in 1058. He was precocious in poetry and misery, for his parents died when he was fairly young, and he was sickly during his short life. He lived for a time in Saragossa, where his patron was a prominent Jewish courtier named Yekutiel Ibn Hassan (d. 1039), a relationship that, though brief, had its ups and downs, as did his relations with his older contemporary Samuel the Nagid, the great Jewish statesman, poet, and rabbi in Granada. Ibn Gabirol wrote panegyrics in honor of other patrons who cannot be identified. As a philosopher, he specialized in metaphysics and logic and engaged in biblical exegesis of a Neoplatonic bent. He wrote a treatise in verse on Hebrew grammar. He wrote poetry both secular and sacred and came to be considered one of the greatest poets of the Hebrew Golden Age. His liturgical poetry was preserved by communities that incorporated it into their religious services and included it in their prayer books.

Ibn Gabirol claims to have written many prose books, but only three, all originally in Arabic, have survived: a magisterial treatise on metaphysics in dialogue form, *The Fountain of Life*, extant in a medieval Latin translation; a treatise on ethics, *The Improvement of Moral Qualities*; and a collection of proverbs, *The Choice Pearls*, now extant only in a medieval Hebrew translation. None of these works has any particularly Jewish content—in Latin translation, *The Fountain of Life* passed for centuries as the work of a Muslim author—and from them, it is clear that Ibn Gabirol belonged to the interconfessional class of intellectuals known in Arabic as *Faylasufs*, people who had a common reverence for the Greek philosophers of antiquity, whom they studied in Arabic translation and discussed in circles of like-minded thinkers, sometimes to the consternation of peers and the condemnation of clergy.

The large-scale absorption of cosmopolitan ideas and intellectual pursuits by Jewish intellectuals and religious leaders was one of the developments in Jewish culture that was made possible by the spread of Islam throughout the Mediterranean world. By the mid-tenth century, most of world Jewry lived in Islamic domains and spoke Arabic as their native language. Through Arabic, Jews had access to the high culture of the age, including, on the one hand, the metaphysics, medicine, astronomy, logic, and mathematics inherited from the Greeks; and, on the other, the vast heritage of Arabic poetry going back to pre-Islamic times and still a living institution thriving wherever Arabic was spoken.

The Judaeo-Arabic culture that emerged found its own characteristic form of expression when tenth-century Jewish grandees in Spain began using Hebrew for poetry designed to function within Jewish society as poetry functioned in Arabic society: as a vehicle for social relations, public discourse, and sophisticated entertainment. A new Hebrew poetry emerged alongside the old tradition of Hebrew liturgical poetry; liturgical poetry also continued to evolve, developing new genres and styles partly adapted from Arabic literary traditions.

Ibn Gabirol came along about eighty years after the introduction of the new Hebrew poetry, at a time when it was no longer in the experimental stage but had a significant body of tradition behind it. Samuel the Nagid (993–1056), about thirty years older than Ibn Gabirol, became one of the most memorable figures of medieval Jewish Spain through his voluminous and very personal body of poetry, in which he publicized his own brilliant public career, propagandized for his points of view, complimented friends, lamented deaths, and celebrated the pleasures enjoyed by himself and his aristocratic friends. It is this personal voice that was taken up by Ibn Gabirol and developed in a more somber, sometimes even bitter, key.

Ibn Gabirol's Poetry

Like other poets of the Hebrew Golden Age, Ibn Gabirol wrote in well-defined genres adopted from Arabic poetry: panegyric, addressed to and celebrating the glamour of patrons and men of stature; lament for the dead, which is partly panegyric in another mode, partly a ritualized evocation of mourning; poetry of complaint, in which a poet lays out his grievances against life or his fellow man; invective, in which a poet excoriates someone in order to damage his reputation. Alongside these more weighty genres are descriptive poems on nature, love poetry, poems about wine drinking, riddles, and epigrams. (Poems intended for the synagogue also fit into well-defined genres inherited from the Jewish communities of the pre-Islamic age.) In non-liturgical poetry, conventions of prosody are rigid: most poems, even long ones, are monorhymed. The rhyming unit is a verse divided into two parts (the technical term is "hemistich"), each about as long as a normal English line of verse. The verse creates the effect of motion rising to a point of highest tension, usually at the end of the first hemistich, and a falling motion down to the rhyme syllable at the end of the second. True enjambment between verses, where a verse ends while a sentence is still incomplete, is exceedingly rare, but a sentence in one verse may be extended by means of additional clauses in the following verse or verses. Accordingly, a poem may feel like a string of verses, or it may seem to be made up of irregular blocks of verses that are somewhat related by syntax or theme or both. Strophic poetry came into vogue around Ibn Gabirol's time, but he rarely used it.

So much for formalities. The emotive potential of this poetry lies in its rhetoric, especially in the constant pairing and balancing of sounds and images, so reminiscent of biblical poetry, though derived by the poets not from the Bible but from Arabic models and though considerably more formalized than biblical poetry. Describing a storm at night, Ibn Gabirol says:

> The night put on black chain mail—
> thunder pierced it with a lightning lance.

He says of a palace in the country:

> It cheers the hearts of poor men, laborers;
> bitter men, failing men forget their want.
> I saw it once and put aside my troubles.
> In it, my heart found comfort from distress.

This rhetorical pairing seems well suited to a worldview in which harmony is the central experience, as exquisitely expressed in a little poem on spring:

> Winter wrote with rains and showers for ink,
> with lightning for a pen and a hand of cloud,
> a letter on the ground in blue and violet,
> a work no artisan could match with all his skill.
> So when earth was longing for the sky,
> she wove upon her flower beds
> something like the stars.

Like human lovers, the sky sends a love letter to the earth in the form of rain, and the earth responds with a gift of embroidery in the form of flowers that seem to reflect the night sky—a perfect expression of the harmony aimed for by the most charming medieval Hebrew poems.

These examples show that Ibn Gabirol knew as well as his contemporaries how to celebrate a world of symmetry, balance, and harmony. But he also knew how to distort the conventions of his age. Ibn Gabirol had a taste for the grotesque that set him apart rhetorically and emotionally from all his contemporaries.

Myriads of poets had written that love or sorrow had kept them up all night watching the stars, but only Ibn Gabirol would write:

> but when I gaze at them all through the night,
>   it seems as if my eyes are loops and they are hooks,

translating the emotional discomfort that keeps him awake into an almost unbearably concrete physical image. Myriads of poets had described relief at the coming of dawn after a miserable night of watching, but only Ibn Gabirol would write:

> and as I watch, the night prepares to shave
>   his head by wetting it with dew,

taking his image from the bathhouse practice of turning dark, stubbly scalp into a shining dome, an image that is certainly expressive but that also discomfits by invoking the toilette. Even when he is describing something that is intrinsically beautiful, Ibn Gabirol is capable of introducing a dark thought. The redness of a rose puts him in mind of

> . . . a girl who runs out screaming,
> her hand upon her head in horror.

A spring shower moistening a garden turns sanguinary:

> . . . the cloud wept,
> sprinkling droplets with an eager hand,
>   as Aaron used to sprinkle blood upon his altar.

This grotesque element figures even in Ibn Gabirol's love poetry, as when he depicts a beloved as having cheeks

> ... white and red, like marble slabs
>   all smeared with lovers' blood,

or when he builds a fantasy seduction scene out of allusions to the biblical story of the rape of Tamar. This tendency comes to a climax in a handful of poems that are completely constructed around such squirmy images. In the poem about one of his ailments, one grotesque image follows another, as he describes the pustules on his legs, swollen with fluid:

> Inside are fetuses that push and shove,
>   until the night gives them my blood to suck.

These images are unparalleled in the Hebrew poetry of this age of classical smoothness and harmony. One of Ibn Gabirol's oddest constructions is a poem describing a bowl of flowers in which the red blossoms and the green leaves are depicted in terms of shame:

> ... like a laughing child whose father slaps him,
>   coloring his cheeks with shame and fear.

Contemplating these flowers, the viewer feels

> ... like a courtier engulfed in plots,
> like a man in panic from a dream,
>   like people who have tripped and cannot rise,
> like a vulture that has lurched into a trap.

(Again, that vulture!)

Other poets of the age wrote poetry in which they boast about their accomplishments and complain about their troubles, but, except when writing in a humorous vein, they never present themselves in a negative light. Ibn Gabirol's personal poetry overturns this convention of positive self-presentation. He presents himself as a sickly, lonely, misunderstood, and miserable outsider; as a man of intellect and ambition that have not brought him due recognition; as a man seething with contempt for his fellow poets and his countrymen. He boasts of his vituperative powers:

> My tongue is sharp as any court scribe's pen
>   to praise a friend, to crush an enemy.

Indeed, his inventiveness in vituperation can be dazzling. We do not know to what extent Ibn Gabirol's complaints are autobiographical truth and to what extent they are a literary pose. Either way, they make up a coherent, if depressing, picture. His most concrete complaint is of poor health, insomnia, and emaciation—complaints that could well be grounded in reality. He also complains about lacking family and loyal, understanding friends. This complaint could be more subjective, but it is frequent. Ibn Gabirol favors a sadly ironic opening gambit for many poems that consists of an imaginary dialogue between the speaker and a friend, as if, in order to be able to speak his heart, he had no choice but to create an imaginary interlocutor. Even this interlocutor, though sympathetic, sometimes berates him for not behaving like a normal person and usually fails to understand him, thus heightening the sense of isolation.

Yet if Ibn Gabirol really was the lonely creature of his self-depiction, this condition could have been partly self-generated, for his insistence on his intellectual and literary superiority and his expressions of contempt for others could very well have rendered a normal social life and collegial relations impossible and patronage elusive. Furthermore, he complains that his writings are not understood and that, to his contemporaries, he is like a Greek speaking a foreign language. Perhaps some of his contemporaries were actually not able to follow, and therefore resented, his specialized philosophical writing. More likely, his peculiar literary sensibility and self-presentation, so contrary to the aesthetics of the age, may have limited his appeal to his contemporaries and stood in the way of literary success in his lifetime.

Where Ibn Gabirol does find a satisfactory interlocutor consistently is in his devotional poetry. He was the first Hebrew poet (as far as we know) to write poetry in which an individual speaker addresses God on intimate terms, thus creating the first body of true devotional poetry in Hebrew (as opposed to liturgical poetry designed for public rituals). This poetry is informed by the profound engagement of medieval philosophers with the soul, which, following the Neoplatonists, they saw as a divine element in man separated from its source in the Universal Soul, and ever yearning to be restored to its supernal place. Many of Ibn Gabirol's devotional poems are addressed to God and are organized in such a way that each verse brings together the "I" of the speaker with the "You" of God. Some of them speak of the soul's divine character and its natural proclivity to express its unity with God or its yearning for such unity. Prayer is sometimes depicted as the spontaneous self-expression of the soul, a verbalization by which the soul proclaims its own divine nature. In such poems, the tension generated by so much of Ibn Gabirol's secular verse, with its harsh rhetoric, finds redress in limpid simplicity of style and in the evocation of harmony between the human and the divine world.

> Three things there are, together in my eye
>   that keep the thought of You forever nigh.
> I think about Your Great and Holy Name
>   whenever I look up and see the sky.
> My thoughts are roused to know how I was made,
>   seeing the earth's expanse, where I abide.
> The musings of my mind, when I look inside—
>   at all times, "O my soul, bless Adonai."

The speaker's view begins by observing the distant, inaccessible sky, then moves closer, to observe the earth, then turns inward to the soul in a smooth motion that echoes the process of emanation from the divine to the material world, and ends with the soul pronouncing the Name of God. The act of contemplation unites the cosmos with the divine spark residing inside man, and from this union emerges a spontaneous utterance of joyful praise. The poem's message of harmony—and its implicit theory of the meaning of prayer—is supported by a perfectly balanced and ordered series of observations, linked by ingenious use of pronouns and sound effects that cannot be reproduced in translation.

The contrast in style between his worldly and devotional poetry confirms what Ibn Gabirol himself tells us repeatedly: that he sees his natural home as the realm of the spirit rather than the realm of men.

Outweighing and outclassing Ibn Gabirol's complaints about his health and his social difficulties are his complaints about the frustration of his ambitions. He aspires not merely to a normal social life but for worldly distinction and fame. He sometimes states this directly, rising to powerful expressions of determination and vehement denunciations of a world that fails to recognize and honor his superiority. At other times, he expresses it indirectly in statements of contempt for worldly honors, loftily rejecting what has not been offered him. The failure of such ambitions is no surprise, in view of his breathtaking boasting and arrogance.

His more weighty ambition is for wisdom, and the most weighty of his complaints are his expressions of frustration about the attempt to achieve it. Whereas to his fellow man, he presents himself as arrogant and superior, to wisdom he presents himself as supplicant. For this purpose, he personifies Wisdom as a beloved female, sometimes a relative:

> Sapience is mother to my soul,
>> Wisdom is my sister.
> She is the one I treasure more than pearls.
>> The world is just my concubine.

And sometimes a lover:

> She brought me to a chamber
>> marble-paved and set with crystals;

> she spread for me her blue
> and scarlet bedding,
> drew me lovingly toward
> her rivers of delight.

Ibn Gabirol's expressions of his determination to achieve wisdom take on the same vehemence as the expressions of his quest for worldly success and honors; it is the same personality, though the objects of the quest seem to us to be opposed.

What is the nature of this wisdom, the quest for which causes him so much exertion and suffering? It is certainly not traditional Jewish wisdom, consisting of the Torah and its rabbinic elaboration, much as these provide the language of Ibn Gabirol's poetry. For the philosophically inclined intellectual, Jewish or Muslim, revelation is merely a particular expression of universal divine wisdom. The object of Ibn Gabirol's intellectual quest is presumably the same as the object set before the disciple by the master in *The Fountain of Life*:

> You must raise your intelligence to the supreme intelligible, strip it and purify it of every stain of the sensible, deliver it from the prison of nature, and attain by the virtue of the intelligence to the highest knowledge that you can achieve of the truth of the intelligible substance, until you are as it were divested of the sensible substance and are in this respect . . . in a state of ignorance. Then you will enclose in some fashion the entire corporeal world in your essence and you will set it as if in a niche of your soul. (3:56)*

But this quest is debilitating. It necessitates resisting the attractions of the material world and overcoming such obstacles to intellectual pursuits as poverty and illness. The quest is also intrinsically difficult, for even the greatest intellect is limited by being encased in a body

---

* Solomon Ibn Gabirol, *The Fountain of life (Fons Vitae)*, trans. Harry E. Wedeck (New York: Philosophical Library. 1962), pp. 127–28.

that is distracted by physical needs and desires. These must be brought under control, the body mortified.

> But know that no one masters mysteries
> until he has consumed his very flesh.

The body is weak; it must be disciplined, controlled:

> ... raging, I berate my heart, and say:
> "Do you dare to give up seeking wisdom,
> too effete to find its furthest limit?
> Trample the cresting waves of wisdom's ocean,
> crack the mountains on the plains of intellect,
> and know that when you come to wisdom's peak,
> I'll order you to count its every grain!"

The enemy in the quest for wisdom is Time, the nearly personified figure representing the hardships and vicissitudes of life; whatever comes between a person and happiness; and death. Against this threatening figure, Ibn Gabirol arms himself as a warrior in order to reach his dual goal of worldly recognition and wisdom. But true wisdom cannot be attained at all as long as the soul is trapped in the prison of the body. Ibn Gabirol welcomes death not just because it will put an end to his pain and sorrows but because of the possibility it affords of fulfilling the inherent desire of the soul for union with the divine intellect.

To a philosopher bent on overcoming Time and conquering his own self in the battle for divine wisdom, how unworthy must have seemed his patrons' preoccupation with wealth, power, and luxury goods, how trivial even their love of poetry, when the poetry they loved consisted of conventional praises and conventional descriptions of flowers and wine, conventional evocations of Eros, all drawing on an age-old and easily mastered inventory of conventional materials. A hint of rebellion at the demands of patrons may perhaps be observed in a panegyric poem that begins with an elaborate description of a palace with its dome and gardens. Little by little, the poet animates the garden, making its birds and flowers and eventually its sculpted gazelles speak and even quarrel among themselves, and then silencing them all with a wave of a rhetorical wand:

> But when the sun rose over them,
>> I cried out, "Halt! Do not cross the boundaries!
> Admit that our noble lord eclipses you,
>> with light as bright as any sun!"

The poet who turned the garden into a chattering, quarrelsome imaginary menagerie can silence the garden, stop the sun in its path, insist that all turn their conversation to praise of his patron. But there is another implication: if the poet has the power to (rhetorically) halt the sun in its course, it follows that he also has the power to halt, refuse, or even reverse the praise of the patron. Without resorting to his usual abrasive straightforwardness but by simply intruding the first-person voice into his fantastic description of the garden, Ibn Gabirol has managed to imply the dependence of the patron on the poet rather than the poet's dependence on the patron.

His irritability toward the great is evident in his gratuitous slap at Samuel the Nagid, also a great poet, though of a diametrically opposed sensibility, when he describes a refreshing goblet of wine:

> The rain was cold as snow on Mount Hermon, as cold
>> as Samuel the Nagid's poetry.

Perhaps Ibn Gabirol's hyperbolically negative self-presentation and his inclination toward grotesque imagery are intended to mock the world of conventional piety, poetry, scholarship, and success; perhaps they constitute his protest against what a philosopher must have seen as the trivial literary scene to which he was expected to conform if he was to make a living from poetry. His descriptions of his loathsome sores, his perversion of the conventional flower descriptions, his warped love poetry, his tortured self-presentation, his outrageous boasting—these may be his angry mockery of the smugness of people who have succeeded in life by conforming to literary and social conventions that come so easily to a man of skill with words. Not for him the easy victories of scholarship or of poetry. He invented his own poetic style, compelled his contemporaries to listen, and berated and belittled them when they failed to understand or to appreciate his work. Ibn Gabirol never tires of praising his own poetry, but in a moment of truth, he describes it as follows:

> I sometimes think God put a thing into my mouth—
> a jewel when He put it there,
> but once in place, it turned into a coal,
> or something like a song, which, sung,
> reeks with a mix of fragrance and decay.

Here, he sounds more like the *poètes maudites* of the nineteenth and twentieth centuries than like his robust and worldly contemporary Samuel the Nagid. If Ibn Gabirol's contemporaries did not appreciate him in his lifetime, perhaps it is because he was not a poet for his time but for our own.

This Book

The present selection of Ibn Gabirol's poetry is by far the largest compilation of his poems that has appeared in English, yet it is not an attempt to suggest the sweep of his oeuvre. It is heavily weighted toward Ibn Gabirol's worldly poetry, especially toward that part of it in which his particular sensibility described above is evident, poems in which he speaks of himself, his struggles, accomplishments, frustrations, and anger. A selection of his nature, wine, and erotic poetry is included not merely to illustrate the lighter genres but as another way of displaying his unique voice. Likewise, the selection of religious poetry focuses on the more intimate kind of religious verse of which he was the pioneer, omitting (with one exception) his voluminous production of traditional-type liturgical poetry. For a complete picture of Ibn Gabirol as a philosophically oriented devotional poet, his great meditation known as "The Kingly Crown" ought, by rights, to be taken into account. I decided to omit this masterful and uniquely Gabirolean literary and religious work because it is too long for an anthology, too well-crafted to abridge, and too recently translated by others.

The translations are based on a careful study of the Hebrew text and the last century and a half of scholarship that has developed around it. The texts are based on standard editions; but occasionally, I chose a different manuscript reading from the one used in the printed editions, and sometimes I found it necessary to emend the text by conjecture. The notes at the end of this volume consist of indispensable explanations of allusions to persons and biblical passages. In order to provide more extensive annotations to the poems than could be accommodated here, I have established a website (http://www.raymondscheindlin.com/ project/vulture/) where the curious reader will find information on the poems' sources, explanations of difficult passages, discussions of textual problems, bibliographies, and summaries.

As a translator, I see my responsibility as being not to write my own poetry but to help Ibn Gabirol's poetry shine in English. The long two-part Hebrew line is generally rendered into blank verse couplets, with each verse of Hebrew appearing as two lines in English. Shorter lines in the translations reflect shorter lines in the originals. But I do not aim in English for the rigid regularity of medieval Hebrew versification. Sometimes a line appears here as three segments rather than two. I sometimes shift the position of phrases within a couplet for the sake of rhythm and replace pronouns with the nouns that they refer to, for the sake of clarity. Where Ibn Gabirol has used unnecessary words to fill in the metrical line, I sometimes telescope them, such prolixity being unnecessary in my more flexible prosodic scheme. I try to mitigate the stop-and-start feel of the long chains of end-stopped lines by linking the verses syntactically where possible. Despite such deviations from the original, I trust that the reader who knows Hebrew will have no difficulty accounting for every word of the English.

I have known and loved Ibn Gabirol's poetry since I was in my mid-twenties. To my youthful self, his grandiosity and self-pity, along with his impulse to insult and provoke, gave perfect expression to the irritability of a bookish suburban teenager during the age of 1950s fatuousness and conformity. As an academic specialist in medieval Hebrew literature, I value Ibn Gabirol as an original in an age that did not particularly value originality and as a cosmopolitan in an age of religious particularism— yet one who was loyal to his ancestral linguistic and literary traditions and moved them forward in his own spirit.

Ambition

וְאַל תִּתְמַהּ בְּאִישׁ כָּמָהּ בְּשָׂרוֹ
לְהַשִּׂיג מַעֲלוֹת חָכְמָה וְיָכֹל
וְהוּא נֶפֶשׁ אֲשֶׁר הַגּוּף תְּסֹבֵב
וְהוּא גַלְגַּל אֲשֶׁר יָסֹב עֲלֵי כֹל.

DON'T BE AMAZED at one who burned to scale

the heights of wisdom and who reached his goal.

He is a soul encompassing the body.

He is a sphere encompassing the All.

וְאִם אַתֶּם יְשִׁישִׁים בִּי תִּמַהְתֶּם
כְּאִלּוּ הַחֲדָשׁוֹת בִּי רְאִיתֶם
וְהַשֶּׁמֶשׁ בְּיוֹם הָאֵל בְּרָאוֹ
בְּאוֹרוֹ אָז וְעַתָּה לֹא יְדַעְתֶּם.

YOU ELDERS stare at me, amazed.

That I'm a thing unprecedented you avow.

But don't you know: the day God made the sun,

it shone as brightly as it does right now?

אֲנִי הַשַּׁר וְהַשִּׁיר לִי לְעֶבֶד
אֲנִי כִנּוֹר לְכָל־שָׁרִים וְנַגָּנִים
וְשִׁירַי כַּעֲטָרוֹת לַמְּלָכִים
וּמִגְבָּעוֹת בְּרָאשֵׁי הַסְּגָנִים
וְהִנְנִי וְשֵׁשׁ עֶשְׂרֵה שְׁנוֹתַי
וְלִבִּי בָן כְּלֵב בֶּן הַשְּׁמֹנִים.

A PRINCE am I, and poems are my subjects;

    a lyre am I for bards and singers all.

My songs are coronets for kings

    and turbans for the heads of courtiers.

I've only sixteen years, not one day more,

    but wisdom like a man who's lived fourscore.

אֲנִי הָאִישׁ אֲשֶׁר שִׁנֵּס אֵזוֹרוֹ

וְלֹא יֶרֶף עֲדֵי יָקִים אֲסָרוֹ

אֲשֶׁר נִבְהַל לְבָבוֹ מִלְּבָבוֹ

וְנַפְשׁוֹ מָאֲסָה לִשְׁכֹּן בְּשָׂרוֹ

וּבָחַר בַּתְּבוּנָה מִנְּעוּרָיו

וְאִם כּוּר הַזְּמָן שֶׁבַע בְּחָרוֹ

וְיַהֲרֹס כָּל־אֲשֶׁר יִבְנֶה וְיִתֹּשׁ

אֲשֶׁר יִטַּע וְיִפְרֹץ אֶת־גְּדֵרוֹ

וְגֵשׁ לוּלֵי אֲשֶׁר תֵּקַד תְּלָאָה

וְיֶלֶד מִבְּנוֹת יָמִים סְגָרוֹ

לְקַצְוֵי מַעֲלוֹת חָכְמָה וּמוּסָר

וּמוֹסַד אוֹצְרוֹת שֵׂכֶל חֲקָרוֹ

וְדַע כִּי לֹא יְגַלֶּה עַד יְכַלֶּה

צְפוּנֵי תַעֲלוּמוֹת אִישׁ שְׁאֵרוֹ

וְקָנִיתִי תְמוֹל שֶׁמֶץ תְּבוּנָה

וְהִשְׁכִּים הַזְּמָן לִדְרֹשׁ מְחִירוֹ

וְעוֹדִי אֶרְכְּבָה לִדְרֹשׁ תְּבוּנָה

וְאִם לֹא יַחֲבשׁ הַיּוֹם חֲמוֹרוֹ

וְלֹא יֶחֱלַשׁ לְבָבִי מִזְּמַנִּי

אֲבָל יָקִים אֲסָרוֹ בַּל הֲפֵרוֹ

I AM THE MAN who cinched his belt,

    not to undo it till his vow's fulfilled,

whose heart turns back in horror from his heart,

    whose soul disdains to dwell inside his flesh,

who made his choice for wisdom as a boy,

    though Time refined him seven times in his retort,

destroying everything he built, uprooting

    everything he planted, breaking down his fences—

a man who would attain (but Trouble blazes;

    Days, Time's minions, block him)

the utmost heights of wisdom and of learning,

    probe the deepest treasures of the intellect.

But know that no one masters mysteries

    until he has consumed his very flesh.

Just yesterday I bought a little wisdom—

    Time was there at dawn to get its price.

Yet still you see me riding after wisdom,

    though Time would never saddle up his mule.

My heart will never flag because of Time.

    It will fulfill its vow, it will not fail.

וְיָגֹרְתִּי מְיֻדָּעַי אֲשֶׁר בָּא
וְלֹא יָבֹא לְאִישׁ בִּלְתִּי מְגוּרוֹ

בְּעֵת לוּנִי וְהַשַּׁחַק נְקִי כָף
וְהַסַּהַר טְהָר־לֵבָב וּבָרוֹ
נְהָגַנִי עֲלֵי אָרְחֵי תְבוּנוֹת
וְהוֹרַנִי בְּאוֹר נָהֹג וְהֹרוֹ
וְחָמַלְתִּי בְּפַחְדִּי מִתְּלָאוֹת
עֲלֵי אוֹרוֹ כְּאָב עַל בֵּן בְּכֹרוֹ
וְרוּחַ שָׁלְחָה בוֹ מִפְרְשֵׂי עָב
וּפָרַשׂ עַל פְּנֵי סַהַר אֲפֵרוֹ
כְּאִלּוּ אִוְּתָה זֶרֶם גְּשָׁמִים
וְתִשָּׁעֵן לְעָב עַד כִּי תְקֵרוֹ
וְשַׁחַק הֶעֱטָה קַדְרוּת וְסַהַר
כְּאִלּוּ מֵת וְהֶעָנָן קְבָרוֹ
וּבָכוּ אַחֲרָיו עָבֵי שְׁחָקִים
בְּכוֹת כִּבְכוֹת אֱדֹם עַל בֵּן בְּעוֹרוֹ
וְלָבַשׁ לַיְלָה שִׁרְיוֹן אֲפֵלָה
וְרַעַם בַּחֲנִית בָּרָק דְּקָרוֹ
וְהַבָּרָק עֲלֵי שַׁחַק מְעוֹפֵף
כְּאִלּוּ הוּא מְשַׂחֵק עַל דְּבָרוֹ

And yet, my friends, the thing I feared befell:

     nothing befalls a man but what he fears.

One night I slept beneath a cloudless sky,

     under a clear moon pure and innocent,

that guided me along the paths of wisdom

     and taught me with its light, teaching as we went.

I was in fear of Trouble, anxious,

     like a father for his son, about its light.

A wind sent sails of cloud against the moon

     and spread its veil against its face, as if

it wished just then to get a stream of rain

     and leaned against the cloud to make it flow.

The heavens dressed in black, the moon

     seemed dead, buried by the clouds,

while over it, thick clouds of heaven wept,

     as Aram once lamented Beor's son.

The night put on black chain mail—

     thunder pierced it with a lightning lance,

and then the lightning fluttered through the sky

     as if to mock its fate,

אֲשֶׁר פָּרַשׂ כְּנָפָיו כַּעֲטַלֵּף
וְעָפוּ עָרְבֵי חֹשֶׁךְ בְּשׁוּרוֹ

וְסָגַר מַחְשְׁבֹתַי אֵל וְחֵפֶץ
לְבָבִי מִשְּׁנֵי פָנָיו אֲסָרוֹ
וְנֶאֱסַר בַּעֲבוֹת חֹשֶׁךְ לְבָבִי
וְהִתְעוֹרֵר כְּגִבּוֹר מִמְּצוּרוֹ

וְכָל־אוֹחִיל יְדִידִי וַאֲקַוֶּה
לְאוֹר סַהַר אֲשׁוּן חֹשֶׁךְ הֱמִירוֹ
כְּאִלּוּ קָנְאוּ עָבִים לְנַפְשִׁי
וְעַל כֵּן מָנְעוּ מֶנִּי מְאוֹרוֹ
וְאַשְׁקִיף עֵת יְגַל פָּנָיו וְאָגִיל
כְּגִיל עֶבֶד אֲשֶׁר אָדוֹן זְכָרוֹ

בְּהִלָּחֵם אֱנוֹשׁ יַכַּת חֲנִיתוֹ
וְעֵת יָרוּץ אֲזַי יִמְעַד אֲשׁוּרוֹ
וְכֵן אִישׁ יַדְבִּקוּ אֹתוֹ תְלָאוֹת
וְלוּ יָשִׂים בְּבֵית נֹגַהּ דְּבִירוֹ.

for like a bat the darkness spread its wings,
>   and when they saw its flash,
>   the crows of darkness fled.

God had shut up my thoughts and blocked my heart
>   on every side from its desire. My heart
was bound in thick cloud-cords of darkness,
>   but it rose raging like a warrior from captivity.

Whenever I have hopes, my friends, and look
>   for moonlight, darkness ruins it,
as if the clouds, for jealousy,
>   are bent on keeping it away from me.
But when its face appears, I gaze,
>   delighted as a servant in his master's grace.

When a man fights, his lance will break,
>   and when he runs, his steps will fail,
and Trouble often overtakes a man,
>   although he makes his home among the stars.

בְּחַר מֵהֲחָלִי מִבְחַר שְׁבִיסוֹ

וְדַי לָךְ מַעֲנַן בְּקֶר רְסִיסוֹ

וְדַע כִּי בַזְּמָן אֵין דַּי לְהַשִּׂיג

סְפִיחַ קַצְרְךָ אַף כִּי שְׁחִיסוֹ

וְהַכֶּרֶם אֲשֶׁר תִּטַּע אֱמָר מִי

לְךָ לִחְיוֹת עֲדֵי תִשְׁתֶּה עֲסִיסוֹ

וְתָרוּץ כַּצְּבִי עַל הַר מְזַמּוֹת

כְּגִבּוֹר בַּשְּׁפֵלָה רָץ בְּסוּסוֹ

בְּמָקוֹם לֹא יָדְעוּ עַיִט שְׁפָיִם

וְאַף רֶגֶל נְמָלָה לֹא דְמָסוֹ

וְיָרַח אַפְּךָ קַצְוֵי אֲדָמָה

כְּאִלּוּ אַפְּךָ רָחָם וּפַרְסוֹ

וְהָיִיתָ כְּעַזְנִיַּת עֲזָאזֵל

וְדָמִיתָ קָאַת מִדְבָּר וְכוֹסוֹ

כְּתֹב סֵפֶר כְּרִיתֻת לַתְּבוּנָה

וְהַתֵּר לֵאוֹת הַבִּין וְקַרְסוֹ

"SELECT one anklet, but a choice one
        from among the ornaments;
        let one drop of morning dew suffice.
There is not time in Time itself to grasp
        your harvest's aftergrowth—
        much less, its after-aftergrowth.
The vines that you are planting now—can you be sure
        that you'll live long enough to drink their wine?
You race like a gazelle on Wisdom's mountain,
        or like a mounted champion on the plain,
places never known to vultures,
        or trampled by the tiny feet of ants.
Your nose sniffs out the universe's limits,
        as if you were a vulture or an eagle,
as if you were Azázel's griffon,
        a desert cormorant, perhaps an owl.
Give wisdom her divorce-writ and be done.
        Undo the hooks and eyes of gnosis!"

עֲנִיתִיו אֵין לְךָ מֵבִין יְקָרוֹת

וּמָאַסְתִּי לְבָבִי לוֹ מְאָסוֹ

וְאֵיכָה לֹא אֲיַסֵּר מַעְלָלָיו

וְעָלַי לֹא עֲלֵי אַחֵר חֲמָסוֹ

וְאֶנָּחֵם בְּיוֹם אֶרְאֶה לְבָבִי

כְּסַבֵא מִבְּלִי יַיִן בְּכוֹסוֹ

וְיָרִים הַזְּמַן אַחֲרֵי פְעָמָיו

כְּאִלּוּ שַׁבְּלוּל הֹלֵךְ בְּתִמְסוֹ

אֲבָל אָרוּץ אֲנִי לִקְנוֹת תְּבוּנָה

בְּעוֹדִי חַי כְּרוּץ גַּלְגַּל וְחַרְסוֹ

וְדַע כִּי לֹא אֱנוֹשׁ יִקְנֶה תְבוּנָה

כְּאִישׁ יִקְנֶה מְעַט כֶּסֶף בְּכִיסוֹ

וְאִישׁ מִלֵּא לְבָבוֹ בֵּין וְאַחַר

יְמַלֵּא מֵעֲפַר אֶרֶץ כְּרֵשׂוֹ

וְאֵיךְ יִרְצֶה לְבַב אִישׁ בַּכְּסִילוּת

וְשֶׂמֶץ בֵּין יְהִי כִסְלוֹ וּמַחְסוֹ

יְהִי כַשּׁוֹר אֲשֶׁר יָדַע בְּעָלָיו

אֲבָל כִּי כַחֲמוֹר יָדַע אֲבוּסוֹ

וְהַמַּדָּע בְּרֹאשׁ דַּרְכֵי אֱלֹהִים

וְהָאֵל מִמְּאוֹר כֹּחוֹ כְּמָסוֹ

וְשָׂמָהוּ כְּמוֹ מֶלֶךְ עֲלֵי כֹל

וְכָתַב שֵׁם יְקוּתִיאֵל בְּנִסּוֹ

I answered:

> I value nothing more than wisdom. If my heart
> > rejected it, I'd turn against my heart.
> Could I neglect to punish such behavior
> > when I, and I alone, would bear the rage?
> Could I not regret to see my heart
> > behaving like a drunk whose cup's gone dry?
> Time plods on sluggishly behind me
> > snailwise, melting as it goes,
> while I run after wisdom all my days,
> > running like the sun among the spheres.
> I tell you, wisdom cannot be acquired
> > the way a man gets money for his purse.
> One man fills his heart with wisdom, while another
> > fills his guts with soil from the ground.
> How can a man be satisfied with folly
> > or hope for just a modicum of wisdom?
> He'd be no better than an ox or donkey—
> > all he'd know would be his trough and master.
> Wisdom is the first of God's creations,
> > and He reserved it from His mighty light,
> made it ruler of the universe
> > and on its banner wrote "Yekutiel."

אֲשֶׁר כַּנֵּס נִתְּנוּ עַל מְלָכִים
וְכַשַּׂחֵק עֲלֵי תֵבֵל פְּרָשׁוֹ
וְרַב כַּיָּם וְהוּא קָטֹן בְּעֵינָיו
וְרָם כָּהָר וְצִפֹּרֶן עֲמָסוֹ
אֲשֶׁר מָשַׁל בְּלִבּוֹ הַלְּבָבוֹת
וְעָשָׂה מַעֲשֵׂה יוֹצֵר בְּחַרְשׁוֹ
וְהָיָה מִפְּנֵי שֹׁאֵל כְּשֹׁאֵל
וְלוּ מֵאֵן בְּחֹזֶק יָד תִּפְשׂוֹ
וּמֵחַפְנָיו תְּהוֹמוֹת יֶסְפּוּ דָךְ
וְהָאֵשׁ נִשְׂרְפָה מֵאֵשׁ הֲמָסוֹ

צֶמַח הַגָּן אֲשֶׁר נַפְשִׁי יְשׁוֹבֵב
וְאֶתְעַנֵּג בְּטוֹב רֵיחַ הֲדַסּוֹ
וְהָיִּיתָ תְּמוֹל מִבְצָר לְנַפְשִׁי
וְאֶרְאֶה הַזְּמָן הַיּוֹם הֲרָסוֹ
הֲקָצַפְתָּ יְדִידִי בַּאֲהָבִים
וְנֶפֶשׁ שָׂבְעָה נֹפֶת תְּבוּסוֹ
וְאִלּוּ נִיב שְׂפָתַיִם יְזוּבוּן
כְּאָמְרִי אָמְרוּ עָגוּר וְסִיסוֹ
וְעַמִּי זָעֲקוּ מִקִּיר אֲבָנָיו
וּמֵעֵץ יַעֲנֶה עַמִּי כְּפִיסוֹ
אֱמֶת כִּי אֵין לְךָ דִמְיוֹן בְּתֵבֵל
הֲיֵשׁ שִׁיר בִּלְעָדֵי שִׁירִי וְאַפְסוֹ

God set him over sovereigns like a banner,
>	furled him like the sky above the earth.
Vast as the sea, but in his own eyes small,
>	huge as the hills, he fits a fingernail.
With his great heart, he rules the hearts of men,
>	shapes them as a potter shapes his clay.
He pleads with beggars to accept his gift;
>	should one refuse, he forces him to take.
His palms pour generosity that makes
>	the ocean surge; his blaze makes fire burn.

O garden where I once refreshed my soul,
>	enjoyed the myrtle's fragrance: May you flourish!
Just yesterday you were my fortress;
>	Time, I see, has torn that fortress down.
Are you fed up with friendship, friend,
>	like someone sick from eating too much honey?
If the swallow or the crane could speak,
>	they'd say the same as I;
stones would cry out from the walls,
>	and knots would cry assent from beams:
"There's no one in the world like you, in truth."
>	But is there any song like mine? Not one!

וְנָזַר מִמְּךָ קֶדֶם אַשְׁרֵי

כָּחַת אוֹ לִבְּךָ הַשַּׂר הֱנִיסוֹ

וְנָעַר מִמְּךָ יָדָיו לְבָבִי

וְאוּלָם עֵץ אֲהָבִים לֹא קְסָסוֹ

לְטֹשׁ עַפְעַפֶּךָ לִרְאוֹת מְאוֹרֵי

וְדַע כִּי מֶרְאוֹת סַגֵּר תְּפָשׂוֹ

וְאִם תִּשְׁאַל לְמִי הוּא זֶה וּבֶן־מִי

שְׁלֹמֹה בֶן־יְהוּדָה הוּא רְכָסוֹ

אֲשֶׁר הֵבַר לְךָ הַשַּׂר לְבָבוֹ

וּבַנֵּתֶר וּבַבֹּרִית כְּבָסוֹ

וְאִם שָׁנָיו שְׁנֵי מִשְׁנֶה לְפַרְעֹה

בְּעֵת נִמְכַּר לְעֶבֶד מִסְּרִיסוֹ

הֲלֹא נָגַע וּבָא עַד יַרְכְּתֵי בִין

וְחֶדֶר אַחֲרֵי חֶדֶר חֲפָשׂוֹ

בְּחַסְדּוֹ דִּבְּרָה צֹעַן וְשִׁנְעָר

וְאֹתוֹ אִוְּתָה לִרְאוֹת חֲנֵסוֹ

וְנַפְשׁוֹ חָמְדָה עַיִשׁ וְכִימָה

וְאַף כִּי זֹחֲלֵי עָפָר וְרִמְשׂוֹ

וְלֹא יָשׁוּב לְבָבוֹ מִפְּנֵי כֹל

אֲבָל רֹחַב לְבָבְךָ הוּא הֱנִיסוֹ

וְאַתְּ שִׁבְרוֹ וְאַתָּה שַׁעֲשָׁעָיו

וְאַתָּה כָּל־מְנָת חֶלְקוֹ וְכוֹסוֹ.

My feet once shied from you, as if afraid,

    or fleeing from your heart, my lord.

My heart once wiped its hands of you

    but never felled the tree of friendship.

Squint if you would see my radiance,

    but know: you might be blinded when you gaze.

You ask the author's name and patronymic?

    Solomon ben Judah is the author.

For you, he cleansed his heart, my lord—

    washed it as with lye or niter.

He's just the age of Pharaoh's viceroy,

    when first sold to a courtier as a slave,

yet he has penetrated wisdom's depths,

    explored her inner chambers one by one.

Egypt and Iraq proclaim his praises,

    Damietta yearns to lay its eyes on him,

while he yearns for the Bear and Pleiades,

    not for the creepers and crawlers of the earth.

Nothing can make his heart recoil;

    yours alone it was put him to flight.

Yet you are everything he has and needs.

    You remain his hope and his delight.

לוּ הָיְתָה נַפְשִׁי מְעַט שָׁאֶלֶת
לֹא הָיְתָה לַיְל וְיוֹם עֲמֵלֶת
אֵיךְ אֶעֱלֹז רֵעִי וּבַמָּה אֶאֱלֹץ
הַאִם אֲיַחֵל נִמְשְׁכָה תּוֹחֶלֶת
הֵן מִדְרַשׁ חָכְמָה בְּשָׂרִי נֶאֱכָל
וּבְשַׂר אֲחֵרִים אַהֲבָה אֹכֶלֶת

לוּ אֶמְצָאָה סִכְלוּת מְעַט כִּי אֵין לָךְ
מַכָּה אֲנוּשָׁה תַּעַרְךְ אֻלֶּלֶת
עַל כֵּן מְאֹד אִיגַע וְלֹא אֶרֶף מְעַט
לוּ מָצְאָה יָדִי כְּבוֹד קֹהֶלֶת
אֶפְשֹׁט לְבוּשׁ תֵּבֵל וְהַדַּעַת לְבוּשׁ
אוֹר לָבֵשָׁה אוֹ כְּסָתָה בִתְכֵלֶת
כִּי מָאֲסָה נַפְשִׁי כְּאִלּוּ נוֹאֲשָׁה
לִי מִמְּצוֹא כָבוֹד וְהִיא נוֹחֶלֶת
דַּלְתֵי יְגוֹנִים פֶּתְחָה אֵלַי הֲכִי
דַּלְתֵי שְׂשׂוֹנִים אַחֲרֵי נָעֲלֶת
מַה־לָּאֲנָשִׁים יֹאמְרוּ אֵיךְ תֶּאֱהַב
כָּבוֹד אֲשֶׁר יִמַּל כְּרֹאשׁ שִׁבֹּלֶת

IF ALL I WANTED were some little thing,
      you wouldn't see me slaving night and day!
How do you expect me to be happy or have pleasure,
      to be content with hoping?—
      Endless hoping makes men heartsick!
Look how philosophy has eaten up my flesh,
      while other people waste their flesh on love!

You think that I should try a little fun?—
      There's nothing quite as sick as hijinks!
No, I struggle on; I wouldn't quit
      for all the honors of a Solomon.
I strip off this world's cloak, while Wisdom
      wraps herself in robes of light
      or gowns of royal blue.
She spurns me, as if she's given up
      on my attaining honors,
      and having given up,
opened gates of misery for me,
      shut behind my back the gates of joy.
What's wrong with people that they ask, "Why care
      for honors that are doomed to wither
      like so many ears of corn?

הֵן כִּי תְבַקֵּשׁ מַעֲלוֹת שֶׁנִּבְצָרוּ
בִּדְמֵי בְּנֵי יוֹם חֻרְבְּךָ נִגְאָלְתָּ

אָמְרוּ לְמוֹכִיחַי וּמִנִּי יֶחֱשׁוּ
כִּי שָׁמְעָה אָזְנִי דְּבַר בֶּן־פָּלֶת
אִם הָאֲדָמָה לֹא תְשִׂימֵנִי לְרֹאשׁ
אֵין הָאֲדָמָה אֹהֲבָה מַשְׂכָּלֶת
לוּ יָדְעָה מֵאֶתְמוֹל רוּם מַעֲלוֹת
נַפְשִׁי לְרַגְלַי הָיְתָה נֹפָלֶת
עַל הַיָּקָר אֶחְמוֹל וְהָאֵל יַעֲנֶה
נֶפֶשׁ אֲשֶׁר עַל הַיָּקָר חָמָלֶת

אוּלַי אֱלֹהִים שָׂם בְּפִי דָבָר כְּמוֹ
אֶבֶן יְקָרָה וַתְּהִי גֶחָלֶת
כַּשִּׁיר אֲשֶׁר יוֹשַׁר וְיָרֵחַ אַף אֱנוֹשׁ
מֵבִין אֲמָרָיו חֶלְבְּנָה וּשְׁחֵלֶת
לוּ כַצָּרֵי הַזֶּה בְּבֵית לוֹט יָדְעוּ
אַנְשֵׁי סְדֹם הִתְדַּפְּקוּ עַל דָּלֶת.

If you go after heights impregnable,

    your sword will end up bloody

    from slashing at the brood of Time."

Tell my detractors

    (and let them hold their tongues in front of me,

    for I have heard the tale of On ben Pelet!)

that if the world does not make me her chief,

    the world does not know who her lover is.

If the world would take my spirit's measure,

    you'd see her on her face before my feet.

I look out for my honor; God will answer

    one who takes his honor seriously.

I sometimes think God put a thing into my mouth—

    a jewel when He put it there,

    a live coal once in place,

or something like a song, which, sung,

    reeks with a mix of fragrance and decay.

If Sodom's men had sniffed such scent

    coming from Lot's house,

    surely they'd have broken down the door.

נֶפֶשׁ אֲשֶׁר עָלוּ שְׁאוֹנֶיהָ

אָנָה תְשַׁלַּח רַעְיוֹנֶיהָ

תֶּהְמֶה וְתִדְמֶה לַעֲלוֹת כָּאֵשׁ

שֶׁיַּעֲלוּ תָמִיד עֲשָׁנֶיהָ

הַאַתְּ כְּמוֹ גַלְגַּל אֲשֶׁר יִסֹּב

עַל הָאֲדָמָה וַהֲמוֹנֶיהָ

אוֹ רַעְיוֹנֶיךְ כְּמוֹ יַמִּים

שֶׁהָטְבְּעוּ בָהֶם אֲדָנֶיהָ

אֵיךְ תֶּחֱזֶה תִקְוַת לְבָבְךָ כִּי

תִבְזֶה מְקוֹם עַיִשׁ וּבָנֶיהָ

אַחַר קְנוֹת בִּינָה הֲלֹא תִרְאֶה

רָאשֵׁי אֲדָמָה אַחֲרֹנֶיהָ

הַט לִבְּךָ מֵעַל נְתִיב חָכְמָה

תִּפְרָשׂ־לְךָ תֵבֵל סְדִינֶיהָ

נַפְשִׁי יְדִידִי נַחֲמוּ עַל זֹאת

אַף נַחֲמוּהָ עַל יְגוֹנֶיהָ

תִּצְמָא לְאִישׁ שֵׂכֶל וְלֹא תִמְצָא

אָדָם יְרַוֶּה צִמְאוֹנֶיהָ

"A SOUL, her outcry rising—
    where does she send her meditations roaming?
She yearns, and in her yearning seems to be a flame,
    its smoke ascending.
Could you be like the sphere, revolving
    around the world and all its throngs?
Or are your meditations like the seas,
    the depths in which the pillars of the earth are sunk?
What expectations do you harbor that you scorn
    the place the Bear inhabits with his young?
Turn away from wisdom's path and watch:
    the world will spread her sheet for you.
With all the wisdom you've acquired, don't you see
    that those the world thinks first are least and last?"

Comfort my soul for this, my friends.
    Console it for its other sorrows, too.
It's thirsty for a person with a mind
    but can't find anyone to quench its thirst.

דְּרָשׁוּ בְּאַלְפֵי הַזְּמַן אוּלַי
בָּהֶם אֱנוֹשׁ יָפִיק רְצוֹנֶיהָ
אִם הָאֲדָמָה חָטְאָה עָלַי
יָרֹק לְבָבִי רַק בְּפָנֶיהָ
אִם לֹא בְּעֵינָהּ רָאֲתָה אוֹרִי
דַּי לָאֲדָמָה עֶוְרוֹנֶיהָ
אִם כָּפְרָה מִמָּחֳרַת פָּנַי
אָשׁוּב וְאֶסְלַח לַעֲוֹנֶיהָ

גַּלְגֵּל אֲדָמָה שׁוּב וְאַל תָּרִים
יַד הַזְּמַן עַל יַד נְבוֹנֶיהָ
רַב לָךְ עֲשׂוֹת עָוֶל וְדַי לִהְיוֹת
אַרְזֵי אֲדָמָה קִיקְיוֹנֶיהָ
הָקֵל נְקַלֵּי עָם אֲשֶׁר מֵהֶם
קַלּוּ מְאֹד עָלַי אֲבָנֶיהָ
וּכְרֹת זְנַב הָאֹמְרִים אֵלַי
אַיֵּה תְבוּנָה וֶאֱמוּנֶיהָ
לוּ שָׁפְטָה תֵבֵל בְּצֶדֶק בָּם
לֹא נָתְנָה טֶרֶף לְבָנֶיהָ
נָחוּ וְלֹא יָגְעוּ וְהִשִּׂיגוּ
רַק מִבְּלִי דַעַת שְׁשׁוֹנֶיהָ
לָקְחוּ בְנוֹת שֶׁמֶשׁ וְהוֹלִידוּ
סְכָלוֹת וְלֹא הָיוּ חֲתָנֶיהָ

Search this generation's throngs; perhaps you'll find
    the one man who could please it.
If the world has done me wrong,
    I spit, with all my heart, right in her face.
If the world has failed to see my light,
    she's welcome to her blindness!
If tomorrow she'd apologize,
    I'd go right back to her, forgive her sin.

Sphere of the world, turn back! O Time,
    stop threatening her sages!
The harm you've caused is quite enough already.
    Too long have cedars been reduced to castor shrubs.
Treat lightweight men with all the contempt they're due—
    I'd rather carry rocks than carry them!
Cut off the tails of those who say,
    "Where are wisdom and her faithful friends?"
If the world would judge such folk as they deserve,
    it would stop providing for their children!
They took their ease, they never struggled—
    inadvertently attained its joys.
They took the daughters of the sun and bred—
    without the benefit of clergy—foolishness.

לָמָּה תְּרִיבוּנִי עֲלֵי שִׂכְלִי

חוֹחֵי אֲדָמָה קִמְּשֹׁנֶיהָ

אִם נִקְלְתָה חָכְמָה בְּעֵינֵיכֶם

אַתֶּם מְאֹד קַלִּים בְּעֵינֶיהָ

אִם נִסְגְּרָה כִּי לִבְּכֶם סָגוּר

הִנֵּה אֲנִי אֶפְתַּח אֲרֻנֶּיהָ

אֵיךְ אֶעֱזֹב חָכְמָה וְרוּחַ אֵל

כָּרַת בְּרִית בֵּינִי וּבֵינֶיהָ

אוֹ תַעֲזֹב אֹתִי וְהִיא כָאֵם

לִי וַאֲנִי יֶלֶד זְקֻנֶיהָ

אוֹ כַחֲלִי אוֹ כַעֲדִי נֶפֶשׁ

אוֹ כַעֲנָק עַל צַוְּרֹנֶיהָ

אֵיךְ תֹּאמְרוּ לִי עֶדְיֵךְ הוֹרֵד

וּפְשֹׁט רְבִידָהּ מִגְּרוֹנֶיהָ

בָּהּ יַעֲלֹז לִבִּי וּבָהּ יִיטַב

כִּי טָהֲרוּ נַחְלֵי עֲדָנֶיהָ

לֹא טוֹב הֱיוֹת נַפְשִׁי כְּמוֹ שֶׁמֶשׁ

שֶׁהֶחֱשִׁיכוּהָ עֲנָנֶיהָ

מִדֵּי הֱיוֹתִי אַעֲלֶה נַפְשִׁי

וּבְעַד עֲרָפֶל שִׂים מְעוֹנֶיהָ

כִּי נִשְׁבְּעָה עָלַי לְבַל אֶשְׁקוֹט

עַד אֶמְצָאָה דַעַת אֲדֹנֶיהָ.

Why do you attack me over wisdom,

you, the thorns and thistles of the world?

Wisdom may be little in your eyes,

but you are quite a little thing to her!

If she is closed to you—because your heart is closed—

I am here to throw her cupboards open.

How could I abandon Wisdom?—God's own spirit

made us allies.

How could she, my mother, leave me? How could I,

the child of her old age, abandon her,

I, an ornament about her neck,

a necklace for her throat?

How can you say to me, "Strip off your ornaments,

and rip the pendant from her breast"?

In her, my heart finds joy and satisfaction

because her Eden streams run pure.

My soul could never thrive if it were like

a sun that clouds have dimmed.

As long as I may live, I strive to raise

my soul and set her dwelling-place beyond the clouds,

for she has vowed that never shall I rest

until I come to knowledge of her Lord!

בְּפִי חַרְבִּי וּבִלְשׁוֹנִי חֲנִיתִי
וּמָגִנִּי וְצִנָּתִי שְׂפָתִי
וְשִׁירִי עַל לְבַב שֹׁמְעָיו כְּפַטִּישׁ
יְפֹצֵץ צוּר וְאָרִיק בַּחֲמָתִי
אֲנִי כִדְבַשׁ וְחָלָב לַמְאַהֲבַי
וְרֹאשׁ פֶּתֶן לְכָל־מֵמִיר עֲצָתִי
לְבָבִי עֵר וְגַם עֵינַי פְּתוּחוֹת
לְכָל־סָתוּם וְלֹא עָרְבָה שְׁנָתִי
וְהִנֵּה הַתְּבוּנָה אֵם לְנַפְשִׁי
וְהַחָכְמָה וְהַדַּעַת אֲחֹתִי
יְקָרָה מִפְּנִינִים הִיא לְעֵינִי
וְהָאָרֶץ לְפָנַי כַּאֲמָתִי
לְמַעַן הִיא כְזוֹנָה שֶׁבְּיוֹם זֶה
בְּבֵית רֵעִי וְיוֹם אַחֵר בְּבֵיתִי
וְעַל כֵּן לֹא דְרַשְׁתִּיהָ וְשַׂמְתִּי
שְׁמֹר חֻקִּי דְּרִישָׁתִי וְדָתִי
וְחֶלְקִי מֵהֲמוֹנֶיהָ לְבָבִי
וְנַפְשִׁי מִשְּׁלָלֶיהָ מְנָתִי.

MY SWORD and spear are in my mouth,
    my lips are shield and buckler.
My poems hammer hearers' hearts:
    they smash, crush granite when I rage.
To friends I can be milk and honey,
    venom to anyone who crosses me.
My heart is always wakeful, and my eyes
    are open ever. Sleep's no pleasure.
Sapience is mother to my soul,
    Wisdom is my sister.
She is the one I treasure more than pearls.
    The world is just my concubine,
a harlot pleased to spend one day with me,
    one day with someone else.
I don't pursue her, for I've made my rule
    to cherish only what is truly mine:
my heart—my only stake in all her treasures—
    and all I own of all her goods—my soul.

נְטֹשׁ לוֹ וַעֲזֹב אוּלִי
וְהַטֵּה אָזְנְךָ אֵלִי
וְאַל תֵּט אַחֲרֵי תִקְוָה
וְדַע כִּי הַזְּמַן כִּילִי

תְּרִיבֵנִי אֲדָמָה כִּי
תְּקַנֵּא בִי וּבְמִשְׁלִי
וְתוֹרֵנִי וְתַרְאֵנִי
אֲשֶׁר רָאוּ מְהוֹלְלָי
וְשָׂחַקְתִּי לְיַלְדֵי יוֹם
וְעַתָּה שָׂחֲקוּ עָלַי
וְאֵיךְ אִירָא בְּנוֹת יָמִים
וְהַיָּמִים בְּנוֹת מִלַּי
וְאָמְנָם כִּי אֲנִי נֶפֶשׁ
וְהָאָדָם כְּמַעְלָלִי
וְאָמְנָם כִּי אֲנִי גַלְגַּל
וְהַכּוֹכָב כְּמַזָּלִי
וְהָאָרֶץ כְּמֶרְכַּבְתִּי
וְאַתָּה מֵלְאוּ שׁוּלָי

34

"QUIT YOUR 'ifs,' and stop your 'maybes.'
　　　Listen to me well:
Don't go after aspirations.
　　　Be aware that Time is niggardly."

That's the world, berating me, .
　　　jealous of my poetry,
instructing me and showing me
　　　the minds of men who mock me.
I used to laugh at the sons of Days,
　　　but today they laugh at me.
Why should I fear Days' daughters?—
　　　My words begot those daughters!
Yes, indeed: I am the Soul;
　　　the human race is one of my effects.
And yes, indeed: I am the sphere;
　　　the stars are constellations set inside me.
The cosmos is my chariot;
　　　my robes' folds fill it!

וְלֹא יֵדַע לְבָבִי רָע

וְלֹא יָגוּר בְּאֹהֳלִי

וְלֹא אָשֹׁם וְאִם אָשֹׁם

לָבִין בְּכִיִּי וְתוֹלָלִי

וְלֹא אָגִיל וְאִם אָגִיל

קְנוֹת רַע בְּרֹאשׁ גִּילִי

וּבִלְבָבִי מְדוּרַת אֵשׁ

וּבִכְבֵדִי וּבִכְסָלִי

עֲדֵי אֶתֵּן לְמֵרֵעִי

וְהָאֵל עֵד אֱמֶת עָלַי

נְדִיבָתִי וְלֹא רָעָה

בְּזֹאת עֵינִי וְלֹא כִילִי

וְאֶתֵּן אֹיְבִי מִרְמָס

פְּעָמַי וַעֲפַר רַגְלִי

וְשַׁתִּיהוּ לְעָמָתִי

כְּכַף רַגְלִי וּמִנְעָלִי

וּמַטָּרָה לְחִצֵּי פִי

וּמַאְכֹלֶת לְגֶחָלִי.

My heart is ignorant of evil.

    No wickedness resides inside my tents.

I don't get sad, and if I do,

    it's only wisdom makes me wail.

I don't make merry. If I do,

    it's mainly when I find a friend.

I have a furnace in my heart,

    in my kidneys, in my liver.

It burns, as God can testify

    till I bestow upon a friend

my gift. My eye and purse

    are never niggardly.

As for my foe—I trample him,

    turn him into dirt beneath my feet,

make him a target for my verbal darts,

    fuel for my hissing coals.

אֱמֹר לָאֹמְרִים כָּלוּ עֲלוּמָיו

וְעוֹד לֹא פָרְחוּ נִצֵּי כְרָמָיו

וְקָצַר הַזְּמַן מִתֵּת רְצוֹנוֹ

וְתֵבֵל מִשְּׂאֵת הֲרֵי זְמָמָיו

וְכָל־כָּבוֹד בְּעֵינָיו קַל וְנָקֵל

הֱיוֹת כִּימָה וְעָשׁ תַּחַת פְּעָמָיו

אֲשֶׁר הָפְקַד עֲלֵי הַר הַתְּבוּנָה

וְשִׁדֵּד אַחֲרָיו עִמְקֵי תְלָמָיו

וְכָסּוּ כָל־פְּנֵי תֵבֵל אֲמָרָיו

וְנָגַהּ אוֹר לְשָׁמָיו עַל לְשָׁמָיו

וְלָכֵן מָאֲסָה נַפְשׁוֹ בְּנֵי אִישׁ

וּמָאַס הַזְּמַן עַד כִּי חֲכָמָיו

וְעַד כִּי אֹהֲבָיו חִלֵּל בְּרִיתָם

וְלֹא פָנָה אֱלֵי אַנְשֵׁי שְׁלָמָיו

אֱמֹר לַפֹּקְדִים עֲלֵי עֲדֵי אָן

תְּרִיבוּן אִישׁ אֲשֶׁר רַבּוּ חֲרָמָיו

וְשָׁכַח מֵאֲכֹל רֶגַע שְׁאֵרוֹ

וְעָצְמוֹ מֵאֲכֹל לַחְמוֹ וּמֵימָיו

ANSWER THOSE who say, "His youth is done
    before his vineyard's buds have blossomed.
Time itself can't satisfy his wishes;
    nor can the world withstand his mountainous ambition.
No honor's good enough for him;
    to tread the Bear or Pleiades strikes him as little.
For he was given charge of wisdom's mountain.
    He plowed deep furrows in its soil,
and now his words have sprouted everywhere.
    His onyx gleams above the heavens.
That's why he scorns his fellow men and shows
    contempt for Time and all the age's sages,
breaks his covenant with his friends,
    shows his back to those who wish him well."

Say to those who nag me, "Can't you stop
    berating someone faced with tribulations,
a man so busy eating his own flesh and bone,
    that he forgets to eat his bread and water,

וְלֹא יִשְׁכַּח לְהַשְׁקוֹת עֵץ אֲהָבִים
וְלֹא יִמְנַע וְלֹא יִגְרַע גְּשָׁמָיו
יְשַׁלֵּם הַיְדִידֹת בַּיְדִידֹת
וְיַמְטִיר אֵשׁ מְלַהֶטֶת לְקָמָיו
וְעֵת יֵחַר לְבָבוֹ בַּחֲרִי אָף
שְׁחָקִים יִרְעֲשׁוּ מֵעֹז רְעָמָיו
וְלוּ רַע יִהְי בַּגֶּד כְּנַחַל
אֲזַי עִמּוֹ מְשָׁכוּהוּ זְרָמָיו
וְגָדַל מִנְּשׂוֹא פֶּשַׁע יְדִידוֹ
וְלוּ מֵאֵן לְכַפֵּר אֶת־אֲשָׁמָיו

וְאֵינֶנִּי כְגֶבֶר יַעֲנֶה־דָּךְ
וְיָשֹׁחַ וְנָפַל בַּעֲצוּמָיו
וְיֶשׁ־אִישׁ יַעֲמֹד לִפְנֵי אֲנָשִׁים
כְּמוֹ כֹהֵן אָדוֹם לִפְנֵי צְלָמָיו.

a man who would not fail to irrigate

    the tree of friendship or refuse it rain;

a man requiting loyalty with loyalty,

    while pouring searing fire on his foes.

When his heart becomes inflamed with anger,

    heaven quakes before his mighty thunder.

If a friend betrays him like a wadi,

    his flood will sweep that miscreant away.

Yes, if a friend commits too great a wrong,

    never in his life would he forgive."

No, I am not a man for soft replies or one

    to flop down on the ground before the great.

Some there are who stand before their fellow men

    like a priest of Rome before his crucifix.

יְגוֹן חֵשֶׁק וְאַהֲבַת הַנְּעוּרִים
עֲזָבוּנִי בְּלִי לֵב בַּיְצָרִים
וְעֵינַי נִפְתְּחוּ מֵעֵין שְׁנָתָם
לְדַלְתֵי הָאֲהָבִים הַסְּגוּרִים
וְשָׁם אֶל כּוֹכְבָיו עַמִּי כְּאִלּוּ
אֲנִי רֹעֶה וְהֵמָּה הָעֲדָרִים
וְנַסַּנִי כְּאַבְרָם הַמְנֻסֶּה
בְּאָמְרוּ קוּם סְפֹר סְפֹר שֶׁאֵין סְפוּרִים

רְאוֹת אֵלֶּה וְכָאֵלֶּה יְדִידִי
יְבִיאוּנִי בְּרָעָה לַקְּבָרִים
צְרָרוּנִי הֱצִיקוּנִי יְגוֹנִים
וְאַף שֶׁבַע צְרָפוּנִי בְכוּרִים
וְהַיּוֹם שָׁת שְׂפָתָיו צוּף לְחִכִּי
הֲלֹא נֶהְפַּךְ וְהָיָה כַמְּרֹרִים
וְחֶצְיֵי הַזְּמַן שִׁירַי וְאִלּוּ
אֲהָבַנִי עֲשִׂיתִים לוֹ כְתָרִים
וְהֵם הָגוּת בְּפִי כָל־הַחֲכָמִים
וּבִלְשׁוֹן כָּל־בְּנֵי מוּסָר שְׁמוּרִים

PASSION'S PAIN and youthful love
  have left me heart-bereft amid mankind,
my eyes unsleeping, gazing
  at the bolted doors of love.
God has left His stars with me:
  they my sheep, I their shepherd.
He tested me like Abraham and said,
  "Count the stars uncountable."

Contemplating images like these, my friend,
  will bring me wretched to the grave.
Sorrows press and pressure me. They keep me
  in their burning crucible to be refined.
A day that touched its honeyed mouth to mine
  has spoiled. Now it tastes like bitters.
My poems are my arrows aimed at Fate—
  if it had loved me, I'd have made them crowns!—
murmured by the mouths of sages,
  treasured by the tongues of cultured men,

וְרֹאשָׁם יִהְיֶה שָׁמוּר לְעוֹלָם

וְיִפְדֵּהוּ בְּכָל־שְׁטָנִים וְעָרִים

אֲשֶׁר בָּחַר בְּשֵׁם טוֹב מִשְּׁמָנִים

וְטוֹב מִכָּל־בְּדָלְחִים וְדָרִים

אֲשֶׁר נִתַּן לְכֶתֶר הַמְּלָכִים

וְלַעֲטֶרֶת וְנֵזֶר מְנֻזָּרִים

וּמָה אַגִּיד בְּהוֹדוֹ הַמְעֻלֶּה

וּמָה אֹמַר וְרַעְיוֹנַי קְצָרִים

בְּשָׁכְנוּ מַעֲלַת שֶׁמֶשׁ וְהָאֵל

הֱבִיאוֹ מִלְפָנִים לַחֲדָרִים

וְאוּלָם מִפְלְאֵי הַשִּׁיר יְעִירוּן

מְזִמּוֹתַי וְנוֹקְצִים וְעָרִים

לְקַבֵּץ מִגְּדוּדָיו הַפְּזוּרִים

וּמֵהַשִּׁיר לְגַלּוֹת הַסְּתָרִים

וְהַשִּׁיר גִּדְּלַנִי מִנְּעוּרַי

כְּמוֹ אָב וַאֲנִי לוֹ בֵּן בְּכֹרִים

וְקָרַן עוֹר פְּנֵי שִׁירַי כְּאִלּוּ

עֲלֵיהֶם מִתְהַלָּתְךָ אֲפֵרִים

וְאֵלָיו יָחֵלוּ כָל־הַמְּלִיצִים

וּפִיהֶם אֶל זְמִיר שִׁירַי פְּעוּרִים

אֲשֶׁר לָנוּ בְּנַפְשׁוֹתָם אֲרָיוֹת

וְהִשְׁכִּימוּ לְפָנָיו כַּשְּׁוָרִים

the chief of whom—may God safeguard him ever,

    save him from his enemies and foes!—

is one whose name is better than fine oils,

    superior to any pearls or crystals,

a man who is himself a coronet, a crown,

    a diadem for kings.

What can I, with a mind so limited,

    articulate of his exalted glory,

when he resides on high beside the sun,

    and God admits him to His inmost chambers?

And yet the miracle of verse stirs up my thoughts;

    they shake off sleep and rise

to muster all their scattered troops,

    reveal the mysteries of song.

For poetry has raised me since my youth,

    it my father, I its firstborn son.

My verse's face emits bright cones of light,

    as if your reputation were its veil.

Other poets long for it, their mouths

    agape as they anticipate my song.

They lie down thinking they are lions,

    wake to learn they're merely cattle next to it,

וּמִמִּשְׂרָה וּמִכָּבוֹד קְנוּיִם
וְלַחֶרְפָּה וְלַלַּעַג מְכוּרִים

אַחֵי מוּסָר מְעַט קַט כַּתְּרוּ לִי
עֲדֵי יִנָּעֲרוּ מֶנִּי נְעוּרִים
וְתִרְאוּ שִׁיר יְבַהֵל רַעְיוֹנִים
אֲשֶׁר בָּתָּיו מְמֻלָּאִים בְּדָרִים
בְּזָהָב וַחֲרוּזֵי הַבְּדֹלַח
בְּמִדְבָּרִים וְעִנְיָנִים הֲדוּרִים
יְשִׂימוּנִי בְּעֵין אַנְשֵׁי זְמַנִּי
כְּמוֹ אַרְיֵה בְּעֵינֵי הַבְּקָרִים.

46

bought away from power and from honor,
　　　　sold to shame, humiliation.

Literary men, give me some time
　　　　to shake off immaturity,
and you will see a poem to amaze your minds—
　　　　its verses set with pearls,
with gold, and beads of crystal,
　　　　splendid both in wording and in substance,
verses that will make this generation
　　　　think of me as cattle think of lions.

עֲטֵה הוֹד וַעֲדֵה וּלְבַשׁ גְּאוֹנִים
וְהִנָּחֵם וְהֶרֶף מִיְּגוֹנִים
וְדוֹם אִם בַּבְּכִי תָלִין וְקַוֵּה
הֲלֹא תָקוּם וְלַבֹּקֶר רְנָנִים
וְדַע כִּי הִנְּךָ יָחִיד בְּדוֹרְךָ
וְשִׁירְךָ כַּחֲרוּזֵי צַוְּרוֹנִים

עֲנִיתִיהוּ וְאֵיךְ אֶרֶף וְאֶדֹּם
וְאֵיכָה יִדְמוּ כַיָּם שְׁאוֹנִים
אֲפָפוּנִי הֲדָפוּנִי מְצוּקִים
וְחֵצִי הַזְּמָן נֶגְדִּי נְכוֹנִים
וִירוּנִי בְּנוֹת יָמִים כְּאִלּוּ
אֲנִי שַׂעֲרָה וְהֵם קַלְעֵי אֲבָנִים
וּבְכַנְפֵי זְמַנִּים יֹאחֲזוּנִי
וְעָלַי נֹסְעִים תָּמִיד וְחוֹנִים
וְאֵדַע הַזְּמָן הֵיטֵב וְהוּא לֹא
יְדָעַנִי אֲבָל כִּי בַיְּגוֹנִים
וְלֹא יָדְעוּ יְלָדָיו כִּי לְבָבִי
מְאֹד חָזָק וְהָיָה כָאֲבָנִים

"WRAP, ADORN yourself in splendor, dress in pride!
　　Be comforted, let go your misery.
If you lie down in tears, be still, have hope;
　　tomorrow you will wake to singing.
Know that no one is your equal in this age.
　　　Your poems are strings of pearls for people's throats."

I answered: How can I be quiet or let go?
　　Can an ocean storm in silence?
Woes surround me, buffet me.
　　　Time's darts are trained on me,
Days' daughters catapult their stones
　　　with hair's-breadth accuracy
　　　at their target—me!
Time grabs me by the coattails,
　　　marches tramping, camping on my body.
I know Time well—though Time does not know me
　　　except in times of trouble—
but this is what Time's sons don't realize:
　　　my heart is obdurate.

וְלֹא יִדְאַג וְלֹא יָשֵׂם אֲלֵיהֶם
וְיִשְׂחַק אִם יְבָאוּהוּ הֲמוֹנִים

אֲנִי הַבֵּן אֲשֶׁר טֶרֶם יְהֻלַּד
לְבָבוֹ בָן כְּמוֹ בֶן הַשְּׁמֹנִים
וְגֵוִי יַהֲלֹךְ עַל הָאֲדָמָה
וְנַפְשִׁי תִהֲלַךְ עַל הָעֲנָנִים
וְיֶתֶר מַעֲלוֹת חָכְמָה תְּבַקֵּשׁ
וּמָאֶסֶת בְּרָב־עֹשֶׁר וְהוֹנִים
וְיָגַעְתִּי בְדָרְשָׁהּ מִנְּעוּרַי
לְמַעַן אַחֲרִיתָהּ מַעֲדַנִּים
וְהִיא הָיְתָה אֲחוֹתִי מִנְּעוּרַי
וּמַדָּעָהּ קְרָאתַנִי בְּבָנִים
וְנַפְשִׁי מִכְּלִי חֶמְדָּהּ יְקָרָה
וְתַחְשֹׁב הַפְּנִינִים כָּאֲבָנִים
וּמֵרֹאשׁ מַאֲסָה נֹעַם אֲדָמָה
וְחַיֶּיהָ בְּעֵינֶיהָ אֲסוֹנִים
לְמַעַן כִּי שְׂשׂוֹנֶיהָ יְגוֹנִים
וּמַדּוּחוֹת וְאוֹנֶיהָ כְּאוֹנִים
וּבָתֵּי מַחֲמַדֶּיהָ הֲרִיסוֹת
וּבָתֵּי מַהֲלָמֶיהָ נְכוֹנִים
תְּפַתֶּה כָּל־חֲסַר לֵבָב בְּיָפְיָהּ
כְּבַעֲלַת אוֹב וְאֵשֶׁת יִדְּעֹנִים

It doesn't trouble itself on their account;

    it smiles when their multitudes assail it.

I am the youth who, still unborn, was wise

    as someone eighty years of age.

My body walks upon the earth;

    my soul perambulates above the clouds,

seeking the highest ranks of wisdom,

    spurning wealth and riches.

I've slaved for wisdom since my youth,

    knowing that its final end is bliss.

Wisdom was my sister in my boyhood,

    and I her favorite among bright lads.

My soul is worth far more than any treasure;

    pearls, to it, are no more dear than stones.

My soul has always scorned the world's delights,

    deemed its life on earth disaster, knowing

that the pleasures of the world are sorrows and deceit.

    Her might engenders mourning.

Her palaces are ruins, but the houses

    that she thought to raze are standing yet.

She leads astray young witlings with her beauty,

    as if she were a witch, a sorceress.

בִּשְׁנוּיָה תְּשַׁנֶּה הַמְצֻקִּים
וְזֹאת לֹא זֹאת תְּשַׁלַּח הַזְּמַנִּים
וְתָשִׁית רָזְנֵי הַיּוֹם כְּמוֹ כֵן
מְחֻסָּרִים בְּדֵעוֹתָם וְשׁוֹנִים
לְקָחָם עַל זְרוֹעֹתָיו וְדַכָּם
וְאִם הָיוּ עֲלֵי חֵיקוֹ אֱמָנִים
וְהָתֵל בַּחֲבֶרְתָם וְשָׂחַק
לְעֻמָּתָם וְהֶרְאֲמוֹ שְׁשׁוֹנִים
רְאֵם עַתָּה אָחִי מוּסָר וּבִינָה
וְהַבֵּט יוֹם כְּלוֹתָם כַּעֲנָנִים
וְיוֹם יֶחֱשְׁפוּ בוֹ רֹגְנֵיהֶם
וְיֵרָאֶה כָל־אֱנוֹשׁ מֵהֶם קְלוֹנִים

חֲמָתִי נִתְּכָה עָלַי בְּשׁוּרִי
פְּתָאִים חָשְׁבוּ כִּי הֵם מְבִינִים
וְאֶשְׁתֹּק מֵעֲדָתָם הַנְּבָלָה
וְאֶכָּבֵד וְאַשְׁקִיט הַשְּׁאוֹנִים
וְהֵם מִתְפָּאֲרִים עָלַי בְּשִׁירִים
וּמִי יִתֵּן וְיִהְיוּ מַאֲזִינִים
וְלוּ הִתְפָּאֲרוּ עָלַי מְאוֹרֵי
שְׁחָקִים הֶחֱשַׁכְתִּים כַּעֲנָנִים

Mutable, she varies men's misfortunes,

> sending one thing, then another,

> arbitrarily.

She turns the princes of the age contrary,

> taints their judgment.

Reared and nurtured in the lap of Time—

> Time took them in his arms and crushed them,

mocked their company, laughed in their faces,

> though he used to give them joy.

Keep your eye on them, you wise and cultured men!

> Watch for the day they dissipate like clouds,

the day their privates are uncovered,

> the day all men will see their shame.

My anger comes in torrents when I see

> fools who think they're perspicacious.

But I do not address that vicious crew.

> I calm my tempests, keep my dignity.

They claim that they outdo me with their verses—

> if only they could even master metrics!

If the stars of heaven claimed they'd bested me,

> I'd turn them dark as clouds!

פְּתָאִים חָשְׁבוּ סִכְלוּת לְהַשְׁוֹת

עֲצֵי עֵדֶן בְּשׁוּרוֹת הָאֳרָנִים

הֲכָאֵלֶּה לְפָנַי יַעֲרְכוּן

צְעִירֵי הַנְּמָלִים הַקְּטַנִּים

אֲשֶׁר לֹא יָדְעוּ בַּשִּׁיר לְדַבֵּר

וְאֵינָם לַהֲגוֹת בּוֹ נֶאֱמָנִים

וְאִלּוּ יַעֲלֶה שִׁירָם בְּמִשְׁקָל

אֲזַי יִהְיֶה כְּאָבָק וַעֲשָׁנִים

וְטֶרֶם יֶלְדוּ כָּרוּ קְבָרִים

לְשִׁירֵיהֶם וְעִמָּהֶם טְמָנִים

עֲדָרִים מָאֲסוּ רֹעֶה אֱמוּנָה

וְלוּלֵי אֵל טְבַחְתִּימוֹ כְּצֹאנִים

וְאִלּוּ נָפְלוּ יָדַי עֲלֵיהֶם

נְשָׂאתִימוֹ וְנָפְלוּ בֵּיוֵנִים

וְכֻלָּם הָטְבְּעוּ בַּבֹּץ צְמִיתָת

וְלֹא יָכְלוּ שְׂאֵתָם הָעֲנָנִים

וְאוּלָם מִפְּנֵי שִׁירֵי יְשׁוּבוּן

אֲשֶׁר יִכָּנְעוּ אֵלָיו גְּאוֹנִים

וְיִתְרַצּוּ לְכַפֵּר הַשְּׁגָגוֹת

וְיִתְוַדּוּ לְהַעֲבִיר הָעֲוֹנִים

עֲרָכוּנִי וְהֵם לֹא יָדְעוּ כִּי

אֲנִי שֶׁמֶשׁ אֲכַסֶּה בַּמְּעוֹנִים

What fools they are to foolishly compare
     the trees of Eden to a row of pines!
Will creatures such as these contend with me,
     those teeny-tiny ants
who can't compose a proper line of verse,
     or even speak one properly?
Even when their verses chance to scan,
     their substance is just smoke and powder.
They open graves for poems yet unborn,
     and lie down to be buried next to them.
They're barnyard animals who spurn a faithful shepherd;
     if not for God, I'd slaughter them like sheep.
If once my hand would fall on them, I'd lift them up
     and let them plummet into mire,
and all of them would drown in muck forever;
     even clouds would never lift them out.
At last, they would retreat before my poems—
     to which the geonim themselves defer—
and beg me to forgive their errors,
     confess their sins and hope for expiation.
They dare compete with me, oblivious
     that I occlude the very sun in heaven.

אֲנִי אֶחְקֹר צְפוּנֵי הַמְּלִיצָה

וְאֶפְתַּח שַׁעֲרֵי דַעַת וּבִינִים

וְאֶקְבֹּץ מִנְּפוּצֶיהָ חֲרוּזִים

וְאֶלְקֹט מִפְּזוּרֶיהָ פְּנִינִים

וְגַבְּנֵי הֲדָרֶיהָ שְׁרוּנִים

לְפָנַי וַאֲרָחֶיהָ נְכוֹנִים

אֲנִי בָאתִי לְחַדְרֵיהֶם אֲשֶׁר הֵם

לְכָל־מֵבִין וְכָל־חָכָם צְפוּנִים

וְאָשִׁיר שִׁיר יְשַׂמַּח הַנְּפָשׁוֹת

וְהַלְּבוֹת יְחַלֵּץ מִיָּגוֹנִים

וְכֹל לֹא יִמְצְאוּ עִמִּי יְדֵיהֶם

וְיוֹדוּ לַעֲצָתִי בַּלְּשׁוֹנִים

וְיֵשְׁבוּ מְקַנְאַי מַעֲלָתִי

מְלֵאִים מֵחֲמַת אֵשׁ הֶחָרוֹנִים

וְאֶת־חַחִי בְּאַפֵּיהֶם אֲשַׁוֶּה

וְאֶתֵּן עַל לְחָיֵיהֶם רְסָנִים

וַאֲשַׂחֲקֵם וְאֶדְרֹךְ בָּמֳתֵיהֶם

וְאַשְׂבִּיעַ פְּנֵיהֶם בַּקְּלוֹנִים

וְיִהְיוּ נַעֲרֹת מִפְּנֵי אֵשׁ

תְּלַהֵט בַּעֲזוּזָה הַחֲסָנִים

וּפִי כָל־דּוֹבְרֵי שֶׁקֶר יְסַכֵּר

וְיָמֹתוּ בְּאֵין כֹּחַ וְאוֹנִים

I ferret out the mysteries of language,

    open gates of knowledge, gates of wisdom,

assemble its disjointed words on strings,

    select its scattered utterances like pearls.

Its humpy hills stretch out like plains before me,

    its paths secure.

I alone have come into its chambers,

    barred to every sage and connoisseur.

I sing a song that makes men's souls rejoice

    and gets their hearts surcease from sorrow.

All of them are helpless in my presence;

    all concede they must defer to me.

Those who envy my superiority

    end up fit to burst with anger.

I get my hook inside their nostrils,

    fix a bridle on their cheeks.

I crush them, trample their high places,

    give their faces shame to eat aplenty.

They become like tinder to a fire

    that blazes and consumes enormous trees.

Every liar's mouth is dammed;

    they die, effete and impotent.

וְלֹא יָרוּם לְבָבָם לֶאֱמֹר שִׁיר

וְאַף לֹא יִזְכְּרוּהוּ בַּלְּשֹׁנִים

וְהֵם לֹא יַעֲלוּ עַל לֵב לְעוֹלָם

וְכַמֵּתִים בְּחַיֵּיהֶם טְמָנִים

לְאֵידָם מַה־שְּׂחוֹק עָשׂוּ בְנַפְשָׁם

בְּשׂוּמָם כַּעֲצֵי קַשׁ קִנְמוֹנִים

וְאָמְנָם לֹא לְעוֹלָם יִהְיֶה אוֹר

כְּמוֹ חֹשֶׁךְ וְחַיִּים כַּאֲסוֹנִים

וְלֹא שַׁחַק יְהִי לָעַד אֲדָמָה

וְכֵן לֹא יִהְיֶה עֵץ כָּאֲבָנִים

וְשִׁירֵנוּ כְּיַלְדֵי אֱמָנָה

וְשִׁירֵהֶם כְּמוֹ יַלְדֵי זְנוּנִים

וְכִי נַפְשָׁם קְרוּצָה מֵאֲדָמָה

קְרָצוּהוּ בְּדָכְיָם מִדְּמָנִים

וְנַפְשֵׁנוּ פְנִינִיָּה וְעַל כֵּן

גְּזַרְנוּהוּ אֲנַחְנוּ מִפְּנִינִים

וּבֹא אָרוּם וְאֶתְנַשֵּׂא עֲלֵי כָל־

מְתֵי דוֹרִי וְעַל כָּל־הַזְּמַנִּים

וְאֶתְגַּבֵּר בְּשִׁירָתִי וְאֶחְבֹּשׁ

פְּנֵי שֹׂנְאַי לְעוֹלָם בַּטְּמָנִים

אֲשֶׁר הֵמָּה עֲרִירֵי לֵב וְרַעְיוֹן

וְאֵינָם שֹׁמְעִים כִּי אִם מְאֲנִים

Their hearts will never dare to speak a poem;

    never even say the word again!

Besides that, no one will remember them.

    Alive, they'll be like corpses in a grave.

They only harm themselves and draw derision

    by pretending cinnamon is straw.

Yet light will not forever be like darkness,

    or life resemble death.

The sky will not be like the earth forever,

    or trees resemble stones.

The poems I beget are legal issue;

    theirs are just a harlot's brood.

Their souls are made of dirt, and being base,

    they craft their verses out of shit;

but my soul is sublime, so naturally

    I've sculpted my own poems out of pearls.

My poems elevate me well above

    the people of my age—indeed, all ages.

Through them I conquer, wrap the faces

    of my foes in permanent obscurity—

men of barren hearts, devoid of thought,

    who never take direction, always balk;

וְדָת אֵל חָשְׁבוּ בָהּ מַחֲשָׁבוֹת

וְשָׁגוּ בָהּ וְהִרְבּוּ עוֹד זְדֹנִים

וּמִתְכֹּנֶת לְשׁוֹן עִבְרִית עֲמֻקָּה

וְקָשָׁה לַאֲחֵי מוּסָר וּבִינִים

וּבִינָה מַפְלִיאֵי הַתְּבוּנוֹת

וְאֵינָהּ כִּי לְחַדֵּי רַעְיוֹנִים

כְּבוּדָה הִיא לְנִכְבַּדֵּי תְבוּנָה

וְאֵין הִיא לַנְּמָלִים הַקְּטַנִּים

אֲשֶׁר אֵין דַּי בְּבִינָתָם לְהַפְלוֹת

צְעִירֵי הַזְּבוּבִים מִשְּׁמֵנִים

אֲהָהּ כִּי הַזְּמַן חָסֵר תְּבוּנוֹת

וְנִמְלָא מֵעֲדַת רוֹגְנִים וְשׁוֹנִים

וְעַל כֵּן כָּל-יְמֵי חַיַּי אֶקֹּנֵן

וְלִבִּי יַעֲשֶׂה מִסְפֵּד כְּתַנִּים

לְמַעַן נֶעְדְּרוּ אַנְשֵׁי אֱמוּנָה

וְסָפוּ כָּל-נְשֹׂאֵי שֵׁם וּפָנִים

וְתַחַת הַהֲדַס סִרְפַּד וְחוֹחַ

וּבִמְקוֹם הָאֲרָזִים קִמְּשׂנִים

וְאִם הִתְמוֹטְטוּ גִּבְעוֹת תְּבוּנָה

וְאִם הִתְפּוֹצְצוּ הָרֵי אֲמָנִים

הֲלֹא טוֹב הַשְּׁאָר נִשְׁאָר וְזָרַח

כְּמוֹ שֶׁמֶשׁ עֲלֵי יוֹם הָעֲנָנִים

who think all kinds of thoughts about religion—
  some wrong through ignorance, some by intent.
The Hebrew tongue is recondite; it's hard
  even for the cultured and the learned;
a marvel among the disciplines,
  suited only for the sharpest minds;
reserved for people of abundant learning,
  not intended for the little ants
who lack the insight to discriminate
  between malnourished flies and fatted cattle.

How sad! This is an age devoid of wisdom,
  full of malcontents and heretics!
I spend my life in mourning over this;
  my heart howls in lament like jackals.
For no one can be trusted any more;
  gone are the men of fame and dignity.
Where once was myrtle, now are thorns and brambles,
  briars where there once were cedars.
But though the hills of wisdom have collapsed
  and the mountains of integrity are shattered,
the best part of the remnant lingers on,
  shining as the sun shines through the clouds.

וְחָשַׁב הָאֱלֹהִים זֹאת לְטוֹבָה

לְהַשְׁאִיר בֵּין שְׁאָר עַמּוֹ אֱמוּנִים

לְשׁוֹבֵב יַעֲקֹב אֵלָיו וְלֶאֱסֹף

פְּזוּרֵי דָת לְאֵל נֹטֶה מְעוֹנִים

וְלִבְנוֹת נִגְדְּעֵי הַנַּהֲלָאָה

וְלַסְאוֹן שֹׁפְטֵי הָרַע סְאוֹנִים

לְנַחֵם לֵב שְׁפָלִים וַאֲמֵלִים

וּמַכּוֹתָם לְרַכֵּךְ בַּשְּׁמָנִים

וְלִרְעוֹת צֹאן מְנֻדָּח בָּאֲפָסִים

וְהָרְזִים לְעַדֵּן כַּשְּׁמֵנִים

אֱמֶת כִּי נִהֲלָם עַל מֵי מְנֻחוֹת

וְהוֹבִילָם לְחַיֵּי מַעֲדַנִּים

וְהִרְוָם בַּתְּבוּנָה עַד לְשָׂבְעָה

וְהִשְׁקָם כִּי הֲרָגוּם צְמֵאוֹנִים

אֲשֶׁר חִזַּק יְדֵי דָת אֵל אֱמוּנִים

וְהֶעֱמִידָהּ עֲלֵה רֹאשׁ הַמְּכוֹנִים

אֲשֶׁר הֵשִׁיב פְּזוּרֵי צֹאן תְּעוּדָה

וְהוֹשִׁיב נַחֲלֶיהָ מִלְּפָנִים

אֲשֶׁר הוֹדַע בְּעַמּוֹ מִשְׁפְּטֵי אֵל

וְאֵלָיו יַעֲלוּ עַמּוֹ נְדוֹנִים

וְכַמָּה תוֹצָאוֹת מִשְׁפָּט יְגַלֶּה

בְּחָכְמָתוֹ וְיַתִּיר הָאֲטוּנִים

God thought it best to leave some trusty men
     among the few remaining of His folk
to turn the sons of Jacob back to Him,
     to gather in the Torah's scattered tribe
     to God Who stretched the heavens out;
rebuild the cut-down, far-flung folk,
     terrify the wicked magistrates,
bring comfort to downtrodden, wretched men,
     salve their wounds as if with healing oils,
tend the sheep, dispersed to distant places,
     and pamper all—the scrawny and the fat.
This man has truly led them by still waters,
     brought them to a life of luxury;
given them to drink their fill of wisdom,
     just as they were perishing with thirst,
reinforced the Law of faithful God,
     set it on the firmest of foundations,
restored the Torah's scattered sheep, secured
     the places of its longtime heirs,
promulgated to his folk God's Law,
     and they in turn appeal to him for judgment.
How many legal problems has he solved,
     and cords untied with his sagacity!—

וְהוּא בַּעַל לְשׁוֹן דָּת הַקְּדוֹשָׁה

וּפִיהוּ הַמְמַלֵּל בַּנְּבָנִים

וְהוּא פָּתַח חֲגוֹרֶיהָ וְחָלַץ

חֲלוּצֶיהָ וְחִדֵּשׁ־בָּהּ יְשָׁנִים

וְיִשֵּׁר מִשְׂגּוּבֶיהָ בְּצוּרִים

וְחָשַׂף מִסְתָּרֶיהָ גְּנוּנִים

וְהֶחֱיָה מִשְׁחָתֶיהָ מְקוֹרִים

וְהֵפִיץ מִנְפָצֶיהָ עֲנָנִים

וְהֶעֱמִיד מִפְרוּצֶיהָ שְׁעָרִים

וְחִלֵּק מַחְלְקוֹתֶיהָ לְפָנִים

נְשׂוּי קָדְקֹד וְלוּ שַׁחַק עֲרָכוֹ

גָּעֲרוּ גַּעֲרַת אָבוֹת לְבָנִים

אֲשֶׁר הַתֹּם וְהַיֹּשֶׁר לְבוּשׁוֹ

וְעָטָה חֲחֲסָדִים כַּסְּדִינִים

וְיָרֵשׁ מַעֲלָתוֹ מֵאֲבֹתָיו

וְיִדִּישָׁהּ בְּאַחֲרִיתוֹ לְבָנִים

אֲבִי הַכֹּל נְשָׂאָהוּ עֲלֵי כָל

וְהֵרִים מִפְעָלָתָיו כִּתְרָנִים

וְהִשְׁמִיעַ כְּבוֹדוֹ בָּאֲרָצוֹת

עֲדֵי אַפְסֵי שְׁבָאִים אַף דְּדָנִים

וְהֵשִׂים אֶת־תְּהִלָּתוֹ בְּפִי כָל־

מְתֵי מוּסָר גְּדוֹלִים עִם קְטַנִּים

that master of the holy Torah's tongue,

    whose mouth is eloquent among the wise

who loosed its warriors' belts, disarmed its vanguard,

    renewed its antiquated parts;

who smoothed its fortified high places,

    uncovered its well-guarded mysteries;

turned its cisterns into springs,

    its desiccated shards to sprinkling clouds;

turned its rubble into gates,

    divided up its varied subdivisions.

His head so high that if the sky would vie

    with him, he'd scold it as a father scolds a son.

Righteousness and fairness are his garment,

    acts of charity his robe of office.

His ancestors bequeathed his rank to him,

    and in due course, he'll vest it in his sons.

The Universal Father raised him over all

    and raised his deeds aloft to be a standard;

proclaimed to distant lands his glory,

    even to Sabea and Dedan;

and put his praises in the mouth of every

    man of culture, great and small alike.

וְאָמְנָם הוּא לְכָל־חַכְמֵי אֲדָמָה
כְּמוֹ שֶׁמֶשׁ וְהֵמָּה כַּעֲנָנִים
וְכָמוֹנִי יְאַהֵב כִּי אֲשַׁוֶּה
תְּהִלּוֹתָיו בְּפִי כַּפַּעֲמֹנִים
יְשִׁירוּהוּ מְתֵי מוּסָר וְיֶהְגּוּ
בְּצִדְקֹתָיו יְמֵי עוֹלָם וְשָׁנִים.

The sages of the world compared to him
      are merely clouds, and he is like the sun.
He loves a man like me because I put
      his praises in my mouth like little bells.
Cultured men will sing of him, recount
      his righteous deeds forever and a day.

זְמָמַי הָה בְּהַר כֶּסֶל נְבֻכִים

וְעֵינֵי יָרְטוּ נֶגְדָּם דְּרָכִים

וּמַה־יִּתְרוֹן בְּאוֹר שֶׁמֶשׁ בְּעֵינִי

וְלִבִּי יַהֲלֹךְ נֶגְדּוֹ חֲשֵׁכִים

וְאֶדְרֹךְ עֹז בְּנֵי יָמִים בְּנַפְשִׁי

וּפָנַי בַּחֲמַת יָמִים דְּרָכִים

וְנִפְתָּה כָּאֲרוּס תֵּבֵל לְבָבִי

וְשָׁדֶיהָ בְּיַד זָרִים מְעוּכִים

וְרַב לִי עוֹד רְדֹף הַבְלֵי זְמַנִּים

וְהַלֵּךְ אַחֲרֵי לִבּוֹת הֲפוּכִים

וְהִתְבּוֹסֵס בְּדַם נַעַר וּמֵאָז

דְּמֵי נַעַר בְּיַד יָמִים שְׁפוּכִים

נָאַם צָמֵא לְמֵי חָכְמָה וְהֹמֶה

וְיָמָיו בַּעֲבוֹת עָמָל מְשׁוּכִים

רְדוּף יָגוֹן שְׂבַע קָלוֹן וּמִדַּם

לְבָבוֹ יִסְכוּ עֵינָיו נְסָכִים

הֲדָפוּהוּ תְלָאוֹת מִנְּעָרָיו

וְחִצֵּיהֶן בְּצַלְעֹתָיו מְעוּכִים

וְרַעְיוֹנָיו יְעִירוּהוּ וּבְנָאוֹת

מְצוּקִים יֵלְכוּ הָלֹךְ וּבֹכִים

"MY THOUGHTS are straying, lost, about Mount Folly,
    with only twisted paths before my eyes.
What good is it if I can see the sun,
    when facing it my heart walks darkling?
In my soul, I trample on the sons of Time,
    while raging Days are trampling on my face.
My heart, deluded, thought the world its bride,
    yet all the while, other men
    were playing with her breasts.
Too long have I pursued Time's vanities,
    gone hell-bent after hearts perverse,
splashed about in youthful blood, such blood
    as Days have always spilled since time began."

Thus says a man who thirsts for wisdom's waters
    but whose days are dragged along
    by ropes of futile labor;
a man pursued by sorrow, filled with shame,
    with blood libations dripping from his eyes,
buffeted by tribulations since his youth—
    see their arrows sticking from his ribs!
His thoughts invigorate him, but they wander
    weeping in abodes of hardship.

וַיִּגַּע לַעֲצֹר בָּהֶם וְיַמֵּי

מְזִמָּתָם בְּדַלְתֵי אַף מְסִיכִים

וְיַעְפִּיל לַעֲלוֹת אֶל הַר תְּבוּנָה

וְרַגְלָיו מִנְּתוֹת אֵלָיו חֲשׂוּכִים

וּמִי יוֹבִיל לְמִבְצָר יוֹרְדֵי בוֹר

וְיָבִיא בֵּית עֲשִׁירֵי בֵּין הֲלָכִים

וּמִילָדִים כְּגִילָם הֵם יְרֵאִים

וְאֵיךְ יִתְיַצְּבוּ לִפְנֵי מְלָכִים

וּבִנְטוֹת אׇהֳלֵי בֵּין עַל יְמִינָם

לְשִׂטְנָם נָגְשֵׁי סִכְלוּת עֲרָכִים

וּמֵהַטּוֹת יְרִיעוֹתָם חֲשׂוּכוֹת

וְהֵמָּה מֵיתָרֵיהֶם מַאֲרִיכִים

וְיַחַד יִקְרְאוּ כֻלָּם בְּשֵׁם אֵל

וּפְסִלֵיהֶם בְּבֵית כֶּסֶל נְסוּכִים

וְאָדֵּם לְאַט עַד בֵּית אֱלֹהִים

וְאוֹרֵם לַהֲלֹךְ בִּמְרוֹם הֲלִיכִים

הֲלִיכִים נוֹסְדוּ עַל קַו אֱמוּנָה

בְּחֻקֵּי אֵל נְתִיבֵיהֶם סְמוּכִים

וְיֶהְמוּן לַהֲגוֹת בָּהֶם וְלִנְגַהּ

תְּעוּדָה מִקְצוֹתָם נֶהֱלָכִים

לְאוֹר עוֹלָם אֲשֶׁר הֵאִיר מְכוֹנָה

וּבִימִינוֹ אֱמָנֶיהָ תְּמוּכִים

He struggles to control them, but they bar
>   their aspiration's ocean with barriers of rage.
He has the daring to ascend Mount Wisdom,
>   but his feet are blocked from entering the path.

Who could lead men bound for graves to safety,
>   bring vagabonds to palaces of wisdom?
If their contemporaries make them shrink,
>   how would they hold up in front of kings?
Beside them, Wisdom may unfurl her tents,
>   but Folly's henchmen rise in ranks against them,
and since they cannot make their tent-cloth reach,
>   they make their cords inordinately long!
All alike invoke the Name of God,
>   while making molten images in Folly's temple.
I shall make them hobble to God's house,
>   teach them how to walk the paths sublime—
paths established on a line of truth,
>   tracks dependent on the laws of God—
so that they long to learn those laws, and to abodes
>   of Torah they will wend their way from distant parts—
a man who lights the world,
>   illuminates the Torah's dwelling,
>   and whose hand supports its devotees,

וְעָלָה מַעֲלוֹת חָכְמָה וְגֹבַהּ

וְלִקְרַאת לַחֲמָיו יָרִיק חֲנִיכִים

לְפָנָיו יִכְרְעוּ אַנְשֵׁי תְבוּנָה

וְתַחְתָּיו כָּל־מְתֵי חָכְמָה הַדּוּכִים

וְהָקֵם עַל לְהוֹרוֹת מִשְׁפְּטֵי אֵל

וְהִצִּיב קַו אֱמֶת לִפְנֵי חֲשֵׁכִים

עֲטֶרֶת כָּל־מְתֵי חָכְמָה וְנֵזֶר

מְתֵי מִשְׂרָה וְחֶמְדַּת הַנְּסִיכִים

אֲדוֹן נַפְשִׁי רְאֵה כִּי יַחֲלוּ לָךְ

וְהִנָּם נִשָּׂאִים נַפְשָׁם וְחוֹכִים

לְפָנֶיךָ לְלַקֵּט בֵּין עֳמָרִים

לְבַל יִהְיוּ בְּסִכְלוּתָם סְבֻכִים

וּבֵין הָעֹמְדִים לִדְרֹשׁ תְּבוּנָה

יְשׁוּ לָהֶם לְפָנָיו מַהֲלָכִים

בְּנִשְׁךְ נַחֲשֵׁי סִכְלוּת תְּשׂוּ נֵס

תְּבוּנָתֶךָ לְהַחֲיוֹת הַנְּשׁוּכִים

וְיוֹם יוֹם תַּעֲרֹךְ נֵרוֹת תְּבוּנָם

וְאַל יִהְיוּ כְּאֵשׁ קוֹצִים דְּעוּכִים

וְיֵאוֹרוּ פְנֵיהֶם בַּהֲדָרְךָ

וּמִבִּרְכָתֶךָ יִהְיוּ בְרוּכִים.

a man who scaled the highest rungs of wisdom,

    unleashed his men against his enemies.

Before him, wise men bend their knee,

    and men of intellect are bowed.

Raised up on high to propagate God's laws,

    he set a line of truth to guide the ignorant.

The crown of wise men, diadem

    of officeholders, princes' jewel,

and my own master. See how they look to you.

    They raise their hearts to you and bide their time

to glean among the sheaves you've left behind,

    so that they not be tangled in confusion.

He grants them access to himself amid

    the throng of those who serve him, seeking wisdom.

When Folly's serpents sting, you elevate

    your wisdom's standard to revive the stung.

You trim their lamps of wisdom every day

    so that they not resemble smoking thorns.

Your splendor is reflected in their faces;

    so may the blessings you enjoy be theirs!

בְּשׁוּרִי הָעֲלִיָּה כִּי

מְאֹד שָׂגְבוּ מְעוֹנֶיהָ

אֲזַי חַשְׁתִּי וְעָלִיתִי

וּבָאתִי עַד תְּכוּנֶיהָ

אֲנִי חֹלָה וְלִבִּי דַל

וְהִיא תָּשִׁיר רְנָנֶיהָ

וְתֹאמַר לַהֲבִיאֵנִי

לְשׂוֹמִי עַל מְכוֹנֶיהָ

לְרִצְפַּת שֵׁשׁ הֱבִיאַתְנִי

אֲשֶׁר סַפִּיר אֲבָנֶיהָ

וּבִתְכֵלֶת וְאַרְגָּמָן

תְּפָרֶשׂ־לִי סְדִינֶיהָ

מְשָׁכַתְנִי בְּאַהֲבָתָהּ

אֱלֵי נַחַל עֲדָנֶיהָ

לְבֵית לַחְמָהּ וּמֵימֶיהָ

וְגַם רֵאשִׁית שְׁמָנֶיהָ

וְאָכַלְתִּי וְשָׂבַעְתִּי

בְּטוּב טַעַם דְּשָׁנֶיהָ

וְהֶעֱלַתְנִי אֱלֵי פַרְדֵּס

חֲבַצֶּלֶת שְׁרוֹנֶיהָ

I GAZED into the upper world,

  beheld her high abodes,

sped aloft until I reached

  her inmost place.

I was wretched, sick at heart.

  She sang to me,

promised she would take me in

  and set me by her side.

She brought me to a chamber

  marble-paved and set with crystals;

she spread for me her blue

  and scarlet bedding,

drew me lovingly toward

  her rivers of delight,

storehouse of her bread and water

  and her finest oils.

I ate her luscious food

  till I was full.

She lifted me into the garden

  of her Sharon roses.

וְנַפְשִׁי חָשְׁבָה לִהְיוֹת

בְּמַנְעַמֵּי מְלוֹנֶיהָ

הֲכִי חָלְפוּ מְצוּקֶיהָ

וְסָרוּ כָל־יְגוֹנֶיהָ

אֲבָל לִבִּי יְגוֹן נַפְשִׁי

אֲשֶׁר יַזְכִּיר עֲוֹנֶיהָ

וְהוּא פָּקֵד חֲטָאֶיהָ

וְהוּא מַעֲלֶה שְׁאוֹנֶיהָ

וְלֹא תִמְצָא מְנוּחָה לָהּ

וְלֹא שֵׁנָה לְעֵינֶיהָ

וְתֵשֵׁב לַיְלָה לִבְכּוֹת

בְּקוֹל יָעִיר יְשֵׁנֶיהָ

וְיֵעוֹרוּ לְצַוְחָתָהּ

וְיָקוּמוּ לְקִינֶיהָ

וְאֹמְרִים מַה־לְּהֶמְיָה

אֲשֶׁר תַּחְרִיד שְׁכֵנֶיהָ

אֲשֶׁר תִּבְכֶּה בָּאַשְׁמֻרוֹת

בְּכִי צִיּוֹן לְבָנֶיהָ

עֲנִיתִימוֹ וּמַה־לִּי עוֹד

חֲיוֹת אַחַר אֱמוּנֶיהָ

נְשִׂיאֶיהָ סְגָנֶיהָ

חֲכָמֶיהָ נְבוֹנֶיהָ

My soul imagined it would stay
    inside her pleasure chamber,
thought her hardships now were over,
    her sorrows done.
But no, for my soul's sorrow
    is my heart: it calls her sins to mind,
keeps her trespasses alive,
    brings her horrors up before her.
She finds no rest;
    her eyes can find no sleep.
She sits up all night weeping,
    rousing sleepers with her cries.
They waken to her wailing,
    rise to her lament,
asking, "What can ail this wailer,
    frightening her neighbors,
weeping through the watches
    like Zion for her children?"
I reply: What point in living,
    with Zion's faithful leaders gone?
Princes, lords,
    wise men, sages,

גְּבִירֶיהָ וְשָׂרֶיהָ

וּמָעוּזֵּי בְחוּנֶיהָ

אֲשֶׁר הֵם כַּצְמִדִים לָהּ

וְכַעֲגִילִים בְּאָזְנֶיהָ

וְהִיא כַלָּה מְהֻלָּלָה

וְאֵלֶּה הֵם חֲתָנֶיהָ

וְהִיא אָרוֹן וְאֵלֶּה הֵם

שְׁנֵי לֻחֹת אֲבָנֶיהָ

מְנוֹרָה הִיא וְאֵלֶּה הֵם

גְּבִיעֶיהָ וְקָנֶיהָ

וְעָלֶיהָ מְעִיל תַּשְׁבֵּץ

כְּרִמּוֹן פַּעֲמֹנֶיהָ

אֱלֹהִים חוּס עֲלֵי נַפְשִׁי

וְהָפֵק אֶת־רְצוֹנֶיהָ

וְהָחִישָׁה מְהֵרָה לָהּ

לְהָשִׁיב אֶת־אֲדֹנֶיהָ

וְאִם אַיִן קְחָהּ אַתָּה

בְּטֶרֶם יוֹם אֲסוֹנֶיהָ.

dignitaries, gentlemen,

    her elite's protectors.

They were bracelets for her arms,

    pendants for her ears.

She was celebrated as a bride,

    they were her bridegrooms;

she, the Holy Ark;

    they, the two stone tablets;

she, the Temple's lamp stand,

    they, its sockets and its branches.

They were like a priestly robe

    hung with bells and pomegranates.

God, take pity on my soul,

    grant her all that she desires.

Hasten to her and restore

    her masters to her,

or just take her to Yourself

    before her doomsday comes.

Sickly Body,
Sorrowing Soul

כְּאֵבִי רַב וּמַכָּתִי אֲנוּשָׁה

וְכֹחִי סָר וְעַצְמוּתִי חֲלוּשָׁה

וְאֵין מִבְרָח וְאֵין מָנוֹס לְנַפְשִׁי

וְאֵין מָקוֹם תְּהִי לִי בוֹ נְפִישָׁה

שְׁלֹשָׁה נֶאֶסְפוּ עָלַי לְכַלּוֹת

שְׁאָר גּוּפִי וְרוּחִי הָעֲנוּשָׁה

גְּדָל עָוֹן וְרַב מַכְאוֹב וּפֵרוּד

וּמִי יוּכַל עֲמֹד לִפְנֵי שְׁלֹשָׁה

הֲיָם אֲנִי וְאִם תַּנִּין אֱלֹהַי

וְכִי בַרְזֶל עֲצָמַי אוֹ נְחוּשָׁה

אֲשֶׁר כָּל־עֵת יְסַבּוּנִי תְלָאוֹת

כְּאִלּוּ הֵם מְסוּרִים לִי יְרֻשָּׁה

וְתִדְרֹשׁ לַעֲוֹנִי רַק כְּאִלּוּ

לְךָ אֵין עַל בְּנֵי אָדָם דְּרִישָׁה

רְאֵה נָא בַּעֲמַל עַבְדְּךָ וְעָנְיוֹ

וְכִי נַפְשׁוֹ כְּמוֹ דָאָה יְקוּשָׁה

וְאֶהְיֶה־לְּךָ לְעוֹלָמִים לְעֶבֶד

וְלֹא אֶשְׁאַל עֲדֵי נֶצַח חֲפִישָׁה.

MY PAIN'S too much, my wounds are deadly.

    My strength is gone, my vigor all depleted.

Nowhere to flee, no refuge for my soul,

    no place where I might find some rest.

Three things have come together to consume

    the little flesh and tortured spirit left to me:

Great sin, great pain, and loneliness—

    could anyone withstand all three?

Am I an ocean or a dragon, Lord?

    Are my bones bronze or iron

that suffering is all around me always,

    my patrimony, as it were,

and You examine no one's sins but mine,

    as if You had no claim on other men?

Just see your servant's suffering and misery.

    Just see his soul, a vulture in a trap,

and I will be Your slave forevermore,

    and never ask to have my bondage end.

מְלִיצָתִי בְּדַאֲגָתִי הֲדוּפָה
וְשִׂמְחָתִי בְּאַנְחָתִי דְחוּפָה
וְאִם אֶרְאֶה שְׂחוֹק יִבְכֶּה לְבָבִי
לְחַיָּתִי שֶׁהִיא מִנִּי קְטוּפָה

יְדִידַי הַלְּבֶן עֶשֶׂר וְשִׁשָּׁה
סְפֹד וּבְכוֹת עֲלֵי יוֹם הָאֲסִיפָה
אֲשֶׁר הָיָה לְהִמָּשֵׁךְ בְּיַלְדוּת
בְּלֶחִי כַּחֲבַצֶּלֶת שְׁזוּפָה

שְׁפָטַנִי לְבָבִי מִנְּעוּרַי
וְעַל כֵּן הָיְתָה נַפְשִׁי כְפוּפָה
וְשָׁם הַבִּין וְהַמּוּסָר מְנָתוֹ
וְנַפְשִׁי הֶחֱרוּצָה שָׁם קְצוּפָה

וּמַה־בֶּצַע בְּהִתְקַצֵּף אֲבָל דֹּם
וְקַוֵּה כִּי לְכָל־מַכָּה תְּרוּפָה
וּמַה־יּוֹעִיל בְּכוֹת עַל הַמְצוֹקִים
וּמַה־יּוֹעִיל לְדִמְעָה הָעֲרוּפָה

MY SONG has been displaced by sorrow,
    my joy is crowded out by sighs.
Whenever I see laughter, my heart weeps
    because my life is being plucked away from me.

—You're just sixteen, my friend! Is this the time
    to weep and mourn about the Day of Gathering?
At your age, better to be swept away
    by one with sun-drenched, rosy cheeks.

My heart has governed me since boyhood,
    subordinated all my appetites.
It made its choice for wisdom and for learning,
    made my appetites its anger's object.

—But what's the good of anger? Just be still
    and hope, for every ailment has a cure.
What use is there in weeping over hardships,
    what value has the tear downpoured?

וּמָה אוֹחִיל וְעַד כַּמָּה אֲיַחֵל
וְהַיּוֹם עוֹד וְלֹא מָלְאָה תְקוּפָה
וְטֶרֶם בּוֹא צְרִי גִלְעָד וְיָמוּת
אֱנוֹשׁ נִכְאָב אֲשֶׁר נַפְשׁוֹ נְגוּפָה.

What good is hope? And how long must I wait?

The day goes on, the term has not been reached.

Before the balm of Gilead arrives,

a man will die whose soul it is that's sick.

כְּשֹׁרֶשׁ עֵץ יְהִי אֹרֶךְ אֲמִירָיו

וְכִתְבוּנַת אֱנוֹשׁ יֹשֶׁר אֲמָרָיו

וְכִמְזִמַּת לְבַב אִישׁ כֵּן יְגוֹנוֹ

בְּשׁוּר טֶרֶם יְבוֹאֵהוּ מְגוּרָיו

יְדִידֵי אָהֳלוֹ תָקַע בְּלִבִּי

וּמוֹרָשֵׁי לְבָבִי הֵם יְתָרָיו

וְנִשְׁבַּע כָּל־אֲשֶׁר יִסַּע וְיֹאבֶה

נָסֹעַ הַכְּאֵב לִתְמֹךְ אֲשׁוּרָיו

וְנָתַן לִלְבָבִי כּוֹס יְגוֹנִים

וְעָלַי הִפְקִדָה לִמְצוֹת שְׁמָרָיו

וְהִפְקִיד הַזְּמַן כָּל־עַצְבוֹתָיו

בְּנַפְשִׁי כַּאֲנִי נֶפֶשׁ פְּגָרָיו

וּפָגַע קָדְקֳדִי בַּעֲנַן תְּלָאוֹת

וְעָלַי סָחֲפוּ גִשְׁמֵי מְטָרָיו

וּפָתֵן הַזְּמַן נָשַׁךְ עֲקֵבִי

וְהָיִיתִי מְשֻׁעְשָׁע לַחֲרָיו

יְמֵי רִיבוֹת יְעָדֵנִי וְהִנֵּה

כְּבָר שָׁלַם וְלֹא שָׁלַם נְדָרָיו

וְכָל אָעוּף עֲלֵי גָבְהֵי מְזִמּוֹת

יְקַצֵּץ בַּעֲדִי כַנְפֵי נְשָׁרָיו

THE LONGER the branches, the longer the roots;

    the shrewder a man, the shrewder his speech.

The wiser a man, the sorrier his sorrows,

    since he sees his troubles long before they come.

Sorrow, friend, has pitched its tent inside my heart—

    my heartstrings are its cords—

and it has sworn to keep pain's feet upon the path,

    wherever pain may go or wants to go.

It gave my heart the cup of sorrow,

    and I am bound to suck its lees.

Time has entrusted all his sorrows to my soul,

    as if I were the soul of all his bodies.

My head, ascending, collided with a cloud of troubles

    and brought a cloudburst down upon itself.

Time's viper sank its fangs into my heel—

    I, who once played blithely by its lair.

Time set a term for days of strife.

    That term is past, the vow still unfulfilled.

I soar above the mountains of the mind;

    he crops my wings,

וְהָיִיתִי כְּמוֹ נֶשֶׁר אֲשֶׁר כֹּל

בְּרוּם יִגְבַּהּ וְיִמָּרְטוּ אֲבָרָיו

אֲנִי אֶשְׂחֶה בְּיָם הַבִּין לְבַדִּי

לְלַקֵּט כָּל־בְּדָלְחָיו וְדָרָיו

וְדַי לִתְפֹּשׂ בְּיָדִי מֶחְקְרֵי נִיב

וְדַי לָלִין לְבַדִּי בֵּין מְצָרָיו

כְּמוֹ חֹשֵׁב אֲשֶׁר יַעַשׂ מְלַאכְתּוֹ

וְכַסֹּפֵר יְחַפֵּשׂ בֵּין סְפָרָיו

וְאֵיךְ יוּכַח אֱנוֹשׁ יַמְרֶה לְבָבוֹ

וְלָמָּה יֹאמְרוּ הַתֵּר חֲגוֹרָיו

מְגוּרָיו קָרְבוּ כִּרְחֹק זְמַמוֹ

וְרֵעָיו רָחֲקוּ מִבֵּית מְגוּרָיו

וְלָמָּה יֹאמְרוּ יִיגַע לְנַפְשׁוֹ

וְלִלְבָבוֹ כְּהָמָס לַאֲסוּרָיו

וְיִרְאֶה הָאֱנוֹשׁ דִּבַּת אֲחֵרִים

וְיַעְלִים עַיִן לְבָבוֹ מִמְּעוֹרָיו

וְאֵיךְ יַתִּיר חֲגוֹר שֵׂכֶל וּבִינָה

אֱנוֹשׁ מֵהָמְרִי פִּתַּח אֱזוֹרָיו

אֲשֶׁר סָגַר בְּיַד נַפְשׁוֹ בְּשָׂרוֹ

וְהִפְקִיד אֶת־לְבָבוֹ עַל נְעוּרָיו

so that I'm like an eagle shedding feathers,

    shedding more, the higher it ascends.

I swim alone in wisdom's ocean,

    gathering its pearls and corals,

nestle all alone in its confines,

    satisfied if I can grasp the mysteries of speech,

like a craftsman at his work,

    like a scribe examining his books.

Why blame a person who defies his heart?

    Why do people say, "Undo his bonds"?—

a man whose fears are near as his thoughts range far

    but whose friends keep distant from his dwellings.

Why do they say, "Let him labor for himself

    and his own heart, once his bonds melt away.

That man sees everything that's wrong with others

    but hides his heart's eye from his own disgrace"?

How can one who has untied the sash of sin

    undo the bond of intellect and wisdom?—

one who charged his soul to tend his body,

    bade his intellect to supervise his youth,

וְנִפְשַׁט מִמְּתֵי בוּז כַּשְׁפִיפוֹן

מְצָאוּהוּ בְּיוֹם קַיִץ מְרִירָיו

וְנַפְשׁוּ גָדְרָה פִּרְצֵי שְׁחָקִים

וְתִפְרֹץ מִמְּקוֹם עַיִשׁ גְּדֵרָיו

דְּבָרָיו מִפְלָאוֹת דֵּעִים וְשָׁת עִם

דִּבְרֵי מַעֲלוֹת שֶׁמֶשׁ דְּבִידָיו

וְקָם לָבוּס כְּסִיל תַּחַת פְּעָמָיו

וְתַחַת פַּעֲמֵי עֶשְׂרִים סְפָרָיו

בְּלֵב יָסֹב עֲלֵי גַלְגַּל אֲדָמָה

וְיֵחָלֵק עֲלֵי שֵׁשֶׁת עֲבָרָיו

וְיָרוּץ כֹּל אֲשֶׁר יִרְחַק זְמַמּוֹ

לְהַשִּׂיג מִבְּלִי הָפֵר אֲסָרָיו

אֲשֶׁר לוּ אִם יְבַקֵּשׁ קֵט הֲנָחָה

גְּזַרְתִּיהוּ וְשָׂרַפְתִּי גְזָרָיו

אֱמֹר אִם לֹא בְּעֵת אוֹכַח לְבָבִי

בְּאַף יִבְעַר עֲשַׁן אֵשׁ מִנְּחִירָיו

וְאֹמַר מִדְּרֹשׁ חָכְמָה הֲתָסוּר

בְּאֵין כֹּחַ בְּךָ לִמְצֹא חֲקָרָיו

דְּרֹךְ עַל בָּמֳתֵי יָם הַתְּבוּנָה

וּבַקַּע מִשְׁדֵּי שֵׂכֶל הֲרָרָיו

וְדַע כִּי בַעֲלֹתָךְ הַר תְּבוּנָה

אֲבַקֵּשׁ מִמְּךָ לִסְפֹּד עֲפָרָיו

who stripped himself of loutish comrades
    like a blasted snake's skin on a summer's day;
whose soul repaired the gaps in heaven's fences
    but burst the barriers of the Bear.
Mind-miracles his words! He sets his chambers
    amid the chambers of the highest heavens,
ascends to crush Orion underneath his feet—
    and underneath the twenty books he's written!
His heart's a sphere: around the earth it rolls,
    encompassing its six directions.
True to his vows, it runs to reach
    the furthest point to which his mind has ranged.
Just let it beg for respite:
    I'd cut it into bits, then burn those bits.
Tell me if my nostrils do not burn and smoke
    when, raging, I berate my heart, and say:
"Do you dare to give up seeking wisdom,
    too effete to find its furthest limit?

Trample the cresting waves of wisdom's ocean,
    crack the mountains on the plains of intellect,
and know that when you come to wisdom's peak,
    I'll order you to count its every grain!"

וְעוֹד לֹא אֶשְׁקֵטָה מֵהַר מְזִמּוֹת
עֲדֵי כִּי אֶעֱלֶה לִטְרֹף כְּפִירָיו
וְלִי עַיִן מְשֹׁטֶטֶת בְּתֵבֵל
אֲשֶׁר מִלֵּב אֱנוֹשׁ תִּרְאֶה סְתָרָיו
וְלִבִּי פָּתְחוּ תָמִיד שְׁעָרָיו
וְשִׁירִי לָטְּשׁוּ שֶׁבַע תְּעָרָיו
וְיָדִי בַּזְּמָן תָּמִיד קְשׁוּרָה
וְאֶקְשֹׁר יַד לְבָנָיו עַל שְׁחָרָיו
וְשַׂמְתִּי מִלְבוּשׁ לֵיל לְבוּשִׁי
וְתָפַרְתִּי כְסוּת כְּכֵסוּת שְׁחָרָיו
וְאָסִיר מֵעֲלֵי עֵינֵי לְבָבִי
בְּהִתָּלוֹת אֲפַר לֵיל אֲפֵרָיו

בְּמוֹת שֶׁמֶשׁ וְקָם לֵיל כְּתַנִּין
לְהָשִׂים עַל פְּנֵי שָׂדֶה חֲמָרָיו
וְהִסַּהַר לְבוּשׁ חֹשֶׁן יְרַקְרַק
שְׁאֵלוֹ מֵהֲדַר שֶׁמֶשׁ וְאוֹרָיו
וְשָׁת עָנָן עֲלֵי פָנָיו לְמַסְוֶה
כְּאִלּוּ יָרְאוּ אוֹרוֹ מְאוֹרָיו
וּפָתַח אָהֳלוֹ נִצָּב כְּנָגִיד
לְמִלְחָמָה יְאַסֵּף אֶת־גְּבִירָיו
וְעָמַד מַעֲמַד מֶלֶךְ סְבִיבוֹ
כְּחֹם אֵשׁ מַעֲרֶכֶת מְנַזְּרָיו

I will not pause until I've climbed the mount

of intellect and torn apart its lions.

I've an eye that wanders round the world

and sees the secrets in the hearts of men.

My own heart's gates are always open wide.

My poems' blades are honed and honed again.

My hand is tied forever to the heart of Time;

I tie Time's times together, white and black.

I've made myself a cloak from night's own fabric

and sewn myself a garment like dawn's robe,

and when the veil of night is hung,

I strip away the veil from my heart's eye.

When the sun expires and the serpent-night rears up

to set its heaps of darkness on the field,

the moon puts on a golden breastplate

borrowed from the sun's own light and splendor

and pulls a cloud about his visage like a veil,

as if to spare his stars, who fear his light.

He stands beside his tent door like a chieftain

mustering his warriors for battle,

or like a king, while ranked around him,

like a blazing campfire, stand his officers.

I will not pause until I've climbed the mount

of intellect and torn apart its lions.

I've an eye that wanders round the world

and sees the secrets in the hearts of men.

My own heart's gates are always open wide.

My poems' blades are honed and honed again.

My hand is tied forever to the heart of Time;

I tie Time's times together, white and black.

I've made myself a cloak from night's own fabric

and sewn myself a garment like dawn's robe,

and when the veil of night is hung,

I strip away the veil from my heart's eye.

When the sun expires and the serpent-night rears up

to set its heaps of darkness on the field,

the moon puts on a golden breastplate

borrowed from the sun's own light and splendor

and pulls a cloud about his visage like a veil,

וְשָׁלַח כּוֹכָבָיו סָבִיב כְּרֹעֶה
יְשַׁלַּח עַל פְּנֵי שָׂדֶה עֲדָרָיו
וְכִרְאוֹת מַרְכְּבוֹת יוֹמָם יְנוּסוּן
וְאִישׁ יִפָּרְדוּ מֵעַל חֲבֵרָיו
וְלֵיל קָדְקֳדוֹ יִמְשַׁח בְּמֵי טַל
לְפָנַי כִּי יְגַלַּח שְׂעָרָיו
וּבֶן־שַׁחַר מְגַלְגֵּל אֶת־כְּסוּתוֹ
כְּאֹרֵג הַיְרִיעָה עַל מְנוֹרָיו
וְלוּלֵי כִי אֲנִי שֵׂכֶל מְשַׁחֵר
וְדַעַת לֹא יְדָעוּנִי שְׁחָרָיו

וְדִמִּיתִי קְנוֹת וּסְפוֹת חֲבֵרִים
הֲכִי לָאִישׁ תְּעֻלָּה בַּחֲבֵרָיו
וְשַׁבְתִּי מִזְּרֹעַ הַיְדִידֹת
כְּקֹצֵר שָׁדְפָה רוּחַ קְצִירָיו
וּמֵרַע קְנוֹת מֵעַם זְמַנִּי
בְּקֶרֶן הַצְּבִי יִתֵּן מְחִירָיו
בָּחַר מֵהַקְּרָב שָׁלוֹם וְהֶרֶף
וְאִם עַזּוּ וְנֶחֶרְבוּ חֲגוֹרָיו
וְדַע כִּי לֹא אֱנוֹשׁ נִצַּל כְּמוֹ אִישׁ
צְרָפוּ הַזְּמַן שֶׁבַע בְּכוּרָיו
יְדוּעַ רָע וְאָזוּר כָּתֳּנוֹת רָע
עֲדֵי כִּי נִמְתְּקוּ עִמִּי מְרֹרָיו

He sends his stars around him as a shepherd
    frees his flocks to roam a meadow.
But when they see the chariots of day,
    they scatter, fleeing, each to his own way,
and as I watch, the night prepares to shave
    his head by wetting it with dew.
A child of dawn furls up his garment,
    as a weaver at his loom furls up his cloth.
No, if I weren't seeking intellect
    and knowledge, dawn would never know me.

I'd thought to get some friends and then some more—
    but does a man get comfort from his friends?
After sowing friendship, I was like a man
    who hoped to reap but found his crops all blasted.
To seek to get a friend today is just to hang
    your purse upon the antlers of a deer.
Choose peace, not war; let go.
    His girded men, though mighty, will be vanquished.
Know that no one can escape unscathed
    except a man repeatedly refined in Time's retort,
a man garbed in such woes, and so inured
    to troubles that their bitterness is sweet to me.

וְאֵיךְ יַמְרֶה אֱנוֹשׁ דַּעַת לְבָבוֹ

וְיִשַּׂח לַחֲצִיר יַעַר וְסִידָיו

וְאֵיךְ אָבֹא בְּלַהֲקַת הַפְּתָאִים

וְהַשֵּׂכֶל הֱבִיאַנִי חֲדָרָיו

וְאֵיךְ אֶלְאֶה מְצֹא פֶּתַח דְּבָרִים

וְעִמִּי נִפְתְּחוּ דַלְתֵי שְׁעָרָיו

וּבָרָא אֵל בְּלִי לֵב עַם זְמַנִּי

וְיָצַר מִבְּלִי קֶרֶן שְׁוָרָיו

וְיָרוּם כָּל־אֱוִיל בּוֹ וַחֲסַר לֵב

וְכָל־יֹנֵק חֲלֵב אֵם מִבְּחִידָיו

וְכָל־נָטָה לְבָבוֹ אַחֲרֵי הוֹן

וְעָבַד בִּלְעֲדֵי שַׁדַּי סְגוֹרָיו

וְלָאֵל יוֹם יְהִי כָל־סַר וְחָנֵף

כְּמוֹ קַשׁ מִפְּנֵי רוּחַ סְעָרָיו

וְיָעֹזּוּ וְיַעְלֹזוּ יְשָׁרָיו

וְיִגְלוּ וְיִמָּלוּ יְהִירָיו.

How can a man of intellect defy his heart,

    or stoop to forest-grass and thorns?

Could I, whom Intellect has brought

    into her chambers, hobnob with a horde of fools?

How could I fail to find an opening for speech

    when eloquence's gates are wide for me?

God has made this age's people mindless,

    made them bulls that have no horns for goring.

Every mindless fool is high and mighty,

    but every suckling thinks that he's elect—

everyone whose heart inclines to lucre,

    all who worship gold instead of God.

God has a day in store when sycophants

    and deviants will be like chaff before His storm,

when all good men will glory in their triumph,

    when the arrogant will be exposed and rot away.

מַה־תִּפְחֲדִי נַפְשִׁי וּמַה־תָּגוּרִי

שִׁכְנִי וְגוּרִי בַּאֲשֶׁר תָּגוּרִי

אִם נֶחְשָׁבָה תֵּבֵל קְטַנָּה לָךְ כְּכַף

אָנָה עֲנִיָּה סֹעֲרָה תָּתוּרִי

טוֹב מֵהֲלֹךְ אָנֶה וְאָן כִּי תֵשְׁבִי

לִפְנֵי אֱלֹהַיִךְ וְלֹא תָסוּרִי

אִם מֵאֱנוֹשׁ תְּנַזְּרִי תֵּעָזְרִי

וּשְׂכַר פְּעֻלָּתֵךְ אֲזַי תָּשׁוּרִי

אִם תַּאֲוַת נַפְשֵׁךְ כְּעִיר מִבְצָר הֲלֹא

תִפֹּל בְּיָדֵךְ אִם מְעַט תָּצוּרִי

אֵין לָךְ בְּקֶרֶב הָאֲדָמָה נַחֲלָה

עוּרִי לְבַקֵּשׁ אַחֲרִיתֵךְ עוּרִי.

WHY SO ANXIOUS, soul of mine? Why so afraid?

    Settle down and settle in, wherever it is you dwell.

You think the world no bigger than your palm,

    but where, poor storm-tossed soul, is there to go?

Better than trudging here and there would be

    to settle down before your God, and never move.

Swear off mankind. Then you will find support

    and see reward for all that you've endured.

If your heart's desire is like a citadel,

    a very little siege will bring it down.

There's nothing in this world for you, O soul of mine.

    Awake! Look to your afterlife! Awake!

מַה־לָּךְ יְחִידָה תֵּשְׁבִי

דּוֹמֵם כְּמֶלֶךְ בַּשְּׁבִי

כַּנְפֵי רְנָנִים תַּאַסְפִי

וּכְנַף יְגוֹנִים תִּסְחֲבִי

כַּמָּה לְבָבֵךְ יֶאֱבַל

כַּמָּה דְמָעוֹת תִּשְׁאָבִי

דָּבַקְתְּ בְּיָגוֹן עַד אֲשֶׁר

קֶבֶר בְּתוֹכוֹ תַחְצְבִי

דֹּמִּי יְחִידָתִי לָאֵל

דֹּמִּי וְאַל תֵּעָצֵבִי

עִמְדִי וְצַפִּי עַד אֲשֶׁר

יַשְׁקִיף וְיֵרֶא יֹשְׁבִי

סִגְרִי דְלָתֵךְ בַּעֲדֵךְ

עַד יַעֲבָר־זַעַם חֲבִי

יֵקַל בְּעֵינַיִךְ מְאֹד

אִם תִּצְמְאִי אוֹ תִרְעָבִי

יֵרַב שְׂכָרֵךְ עַד מְאֹד

וּבְאַחֲרִיתֵךְ תֵּיטְבִי

הִנָּזְרִי מֵאַחֲרֵי

תֵבֵל וְאַל תִּתְעָרְבִי

WHAT KEEPS you sitting, O my soul,

  silent, like a captive king,

dragging wings of sorrow,

  your song-wings folded?

How long will you grieve,

  how long pour tears?

You've clung to sorrow long enough

  to dig a grave inside yourself!

Wait quietly for God, my soul,

  wait quietly, and don't be sad.

Stay put and live in hope until

  He-Who-Dwells-on-High takes notice.

Shut your door against the world,

  take cover till the rage-storm passes.

Are you hungry? Are you thirsty?

  Take it lightly, don't be troubled.

Ultimately, you will prosper.

  Yours will be reward abundant.

Only swear to shun the world.

  Don't involve yourself with her!

מַה־לָּךְ אֲדָמָה בְּגָדָה

תִּתְהַלְּכִי וּתְסוֹבָבִי

נַפְשִׁי בְּיָדֵךְ מָאֲסָה

לַשָּׁוְא עָלַי תַּעְגָּבִי

אַל תִּתְּנִי כִּי מָחֳרָת

תִּקְחִי אֲשֶׁר תִּתְנַדָּבִי

שׁוּבִי יְחִידָתִי לָאֵל

שׁוּבִי וְלִבֵּךְ שׁוֹבָבִי

הִתְחַנְּנִי אֵלָיו וְגַם

דִּמְעָה לְפָנָיו שַׁאֲבִי

אוּלַי יְצַו וְיִשְׁלָחֵךְ

מִבּוֹר אֲשֶׁר בּוֹ תִשְׁכְּבִי

מִבֵּין אֲנָשִׁים בְּעָרִים

שֶׁתִּשְׂנְאִי וּתְתַעֲבִי

אִם תִּכְתְּבִי לֹא יֵדְעוּ

אִם תִּמְחֲקִי אוֹ תִכְתְּבִי

אִם תֹּאמְרִי לֹא יֵדְעוּ

אִם תִּצְדְּקִי אוֹ תִכְזְבִי

יוֹם תֵּצְאִי מֵהֶם תְּנִי

תּוֹדָה וְזֶבַח קָרְבִי

יוֹם תֵּצְאִי לִרְאוֹת אֱנוֹשׁ

אָז כָּאֱנוֹשׁ תִּתְחַשְּׁבִי

Faithless world, you're always wandering,
     roaming restlessly—but why?
I despise your so-called beauty.
     A waste of time to flirt with me!
You can keep your gifts; tomorrow
     you would only take them back.

Back, my soul, return to God.
     Go back, turn your heart to Him.
Supplicate Him, pour your tears,
     bucketfuls of tears to Him—
Maybe He will liberate you
     from the prison where you lie,
from among the ignorant—
men you hate, men you despise.
If you write, they can't tell whether
     you are writing or erasing.
If you speak, they don't know whether
     you are speaking truth or lies.
The day you see the last of them,
     give thanks with offerings to God!
When you escape and mix with humans,
     only then will you feel human!

קוּמִי עֲנִיָּה סֹעֲרָה

קוּמִי וְגַם הִתְיַצְּבִי

קוּמִי וְגוּרִי בַּאֲשֶׁר

תֵּדְעִי תִּנָּקְבִי

קוּמִי וְשִׁכְחִי אָב וָאֵם

צוּרֵךְ לְבַדּוֹ אֱהֲבִי

קוּמִי וְרוּצִי אַחֲרָיו

קַלָּה כְּנֶשֶׁר אוֹ צְבִי

אִם תִּמְצָאִי מָצוֹק וְצַר

אַל תִּפְחֲדִי אַל תִּרְהֲבִי

אִם תִּדְרְכִי עֵמֶק וְהַר

אִם בָּמֳתֵי יָם תִּרְכְּבִי

שִׁימִי סְפָרַד אַחֲרֵי

גֵּוֵךְ וְאַל תִּתְעַכְּבִי

עַד תִּדְרְכִי צֹעַן וְגַם

בָּבֶל וְאֶרֶץ הַצְּבִי

שָׁם תִּדְרְכִי כָּל־עֹז וְשָׁם

תִּנָּשְׂאִי תִּשְׂגְּבִי

לָמָה עֲנִיָּה סֹעֲרָה

תִּכְלִי וְלָמָה תִדְאֲבִי

הַעַל נְטֹשׁ עַמֵּךְ וְאִם

עַל בֵּית מְגוּרֵךְ תִּדְאֲבִי

Arise, my wretched, storm-tossed soul.

    Rise up, go forth boldly.

Arise! Go and live wherever

    you can gain a name and fame.

Arise! Forget your parents,

    give your love to God alone.

Arise and run to follow Him

    swift as a gazelle, an eagle.

Should you meet with hardship, hatred,

    do not fear or be dismayed,

even treading valleys, mountains,

    even riding ocean's crests.

Put al-Andalus behind your back,

    never hesitate

until you tread Iraq and Egypt,

    until you reach the Land of Beauty.

There you'll strut in glory.

    There you'll reach the heights of fame.

Why, my wretched, storm-tossed soul,

    do you languish, do you sorrow?

Are you aching for your people,

    for your homeland left behind?

שִׂימִי שְׁתֵּי אֵלֶּה לְמוּל
עֵינֵךְ וְאָז לֹא תִכְאֲבִי
כִּי צֵל אֱלוֹהַּ בַּעֲדֵךְ
אִם תֵּלְכִי אוֹ תֵשְׁבִי
כִּי גֵר אֲנִי נֶחְשָׁב עֲדֵי
עַצְמִי בְּקֶבֶר תִּרְקְבִי
זִכְרִי שְׁלֹשָׁה נִתְּנוּ
לָגוּר וּבָהֶם חַשְׁבִי
אֵיתָן וְאִישׁ תָּמִים וְצִיר
נָס מִפְּנֵי יַד אֹיְבִי
חָסוּ בְּגָלוּתָם בְּשֵׁם
צוּר בַּעֲרָבוֹת רֹכְבִי

אֶרֶץ יְרִיבַי אַחֲרֵי
תֹּאַר בְּקִלְלַת בֶּן־לִבִּי
גָּפְרִית וְגַם מֶלַח וָאֵשׁ
תֹּאכַל יְבוּלָהּ בַּעֲבִי
אִי לָךְ אֶרֶץ שׁוֹרְרֵי
יוֹם אַחֲרֵי תַעַזְבִי
אֵין לִי בְּקִרְבֵּךְ נַחֲלָה
אִם תֵּצְרִי אוֹ תִרְחֲבִי
תַּאֲוַת לְבָבִי לַנֻּדָּד
עַד אָן וּמָתַי תִּקְרְבִי

Keep two thoughts before your eyes;
　　all your pain will go away:
First, God's shadow will protect you
　　whether you depart or stay.
Second, you are just a stranger
　　till your bones rot in the ground.
Think of three men who were fated
　　to wander. Meditate on them:
Faithful Abraham, Jacob the Innocent,
　　and Moses, Messenger of God, who fled his foe.
All were exiled, all took shelter
　　in the Lord Who rides the heavens.

Land of my enemies, I leave you
　　with the curse of Ben-Levi:
May sulfur, salt, and conflagration
　　destroy your produce in the ground.
Woe befall you once I'm gone,
　　land of men who glare at me.
I renounce my share of you,
　　whether you decline or prosper.
All I want is to get out!
　　But when? How long must I wait?

הֵן בֵּין שְׁוָרִים נֶאֱסַר

להפהֵ עלי מא חל בי

להפהֵ עלי קום גﬞדו

לם ישערו מארבי

להפהֵ עלי מכתﬞי בהם

ועלי עטים תנשﬞבי

להפהֵ עלי זמאן אבי

קד טאל פיה תעגﬞבי

להפהֵ עלי סקע אלדﬞי

צﬞאק פיה מטלבי

בקית פיה מפרדא

חתי אסתבﬞד תגﬞרבי

חל אלגﬞפא מקאלתי

אללה יעלם מדﬞהבי.

Just look at me, tied to these oxen!

    Ah! What has become of me!

Ah! How rich these people are;

    they can't imagine my ambition!

Ah! Too long I've been among them,

    How entangled I've become!

Ah! Time is a stubborn thing!

    How long has it kept me in horror!

Ah! That region simply is

    too small for what I crave!

I've been left here all alone,

    with no choice but to wander on.

How coarse has my speech become!

    But God knows what I mean to say.

נִחַר בְּקָרְאִי גְּרוֹנִי

דָּבַק לְחִכִּי לְשׁוֹנִי

הָיָה לְבָבִי סְחַרְחַר

מֵרֹב כְּאֵבִי וְאוֹנִי

גָּדַל יְגוֹנִי וְחָדַל

מִתֵּת תְּנוּמָה לְעֵינִי

כַּמָּה אֲיַחֵל וְכַמָּה

יִבְעַר כְּמוֹ אֵשׁ חֲרוֹנִי

עַל מִי אֲדַבֵּר וְאָעִיד

וּלְמִי אֲסַפֵּר יְגוֹנִי

לוּ יֵשׁ מְנַחֵם מְרַחֵם

עָלַי וְיֹאחֵז יְמִינִי

אֶשְׁפֹּךְ לְפָנָיו לְבָבִי

אַגִּיד קְצֵה עִצְּבוֹנִי

אוּלַי בְּזָכְרִי יְגוֹנִי

אֶשְׁקֹט מְעַט מִשְּׂאוֹנִי

שְׁאַל שְׁלוֹמִי קְרַב נָא

וּשְׁמַע כְּמוֹ יָם הֲמוֹנִי

אִם יֵשׁ לְבָבְךָ כְּשָׁמִיר

יֵרַךְ לְרֹב דִּרְאוֹנִי

MY THROAT is all inflamed with crying,
    my tongue is sticking to my mouth,
my heart is spinning, dizzy
    with all this pain and grief,
so far gone in misery,
    my eyes refuse to close for sleep.
How long must I hold on to hope?
    How long must my anger burn?
Who is there to tell what I've been through,
    to whom can I explain my pain?
If there were someone here to comfort me,
    to take my hand in pity,
I'd pour my heart out for him to hear.
    I'd tell him of my sorrows.
Maybe speaking of my troubles
    would bring me some relief from horror.

You ask me how I am? Just come
    and hear my oceanic roar.
Even a heart of rock would soften
    to learn how I'm reviled.

אֵיךְ תַּחֲשֹׁב כִּי אֲנִי חַי

עַל דַּעְתְּךָ דַּאֲבוֹנִי

הֲמְעַט הֱיוֹתִי בְּתוֹךְ עַם

יַחְשֹׁב שְׂמֹאלוֹ יְמִינִי

נִקְבָּר אֲבָל לֹא בַמִּדְבָּר

כִּי אִם בְּבֵיתִי אֲרוֹנִי

נִכְאָב בְּלִי אֵם וְלֹא אָב

צָעִיר וְיָחִיד וְעָנִי

נִפְרָד בְּלִי אָח וְאֵין לִי

רֵעַ לְבַד רַעְיוֹנִי

אֶמְסֹךְ בְּדָמִי דְמָעַי

אֶמְסֹךְ דְּמָעַי בְּיֵינִי

אֶצְמָא לְרֵעַ וְאֶכְלֶה

טֶרֶם כְּלוֹת צִמְאוֹנִי

כְּאִלּוּ שְׁחָקִים וְחֵילָם

בֵּין תַּאֲוָתִי וּבֵינִי

נֶחְשָׁב כְּמוֹ גֵר וְתוֹשָׁב

יוֹשֵׁב כְּשֶׁבֶת יְעֵנִי

בֵּין כָּל־פְּתַלְתֹּל וְסָכָל

לִבּוֹ כְּלֵב תַּחְכְּמֹנִי

זֶה יִשְׁקֵךְ רֹאשׁ פְּתָנִים

זֶה יַחֲלִיק רֹאשׁ וְיָנִי

If you knew how I suffer, you would wonder
        what it is that keeps me going on with life.
Is it nothing that I live among a people
        incapable of telling right from left?
That I'm buried, but not in any graveyard:
        my own house is my coffin!
In pain, without a mother or a father;
        alone, a boy, a pauper,
on my own, without even a brother.
        Nothing but my own thoughts for companions.
I mix my tears with my blood,
        I mix my wine with my tears.
I'm thirsting for a friend but know I'll die
        before I slake that thirst.
You'd think that the sky and its orbs
        stood between me and the thing that I long for.
I feel like a stranger, a transient,
        making my home with the ostriches,
twisted, ignorant folk
        (every one sure he's a sage).
One gives you venom to drink;
        one pats your head and then cracks it.

יָשִׂים אָרְבּוֹ בְּקִרְבּוֹ

יֹאמַר לְךָ בִּי אֲדֹנִי

עַם נִמְאֲסוּ לִי אֲבֹתָם

מִהְיוֹת כְּלָבִים לְצֹאנִי

לֹא יַאֲדִימוּ פְנֵיהֶם

כִּי אִם צְבָעוּם בְּשָׁנִי

הֵם כַּעֲנָקִים בְּעֵינָם

הֵם כַּחֲגָבִים בְּעֵינִי

בִּשְׂאֵת מְשָׁלַי יְרִיבוּן

עַמִּי כְּמוֹ עַם יְוָנִי

דִּבֶּר שְׂפַת עַם וְנִשְׁמַע

כִּי זֶה לְשׁוֹן אַשְׁקְלוֹנִי

עַתָּה אֲדַקֵּם כְּמוֹ טִיט

כִּי קַלְּשׁוֹנִי לְשׁוֹנִי

אִם אָזְנְכֶם הִיא עֲרֵלָה

מַה־יַּעֲשֶׂה פַּעֲמֹנִי

לֹא יוּכְלוּ צַוְּארֵיכֶם

לָשֵׂאת זְהַב שַׁהֲרֹנִי

לוּ פָעֲרוּ הַפְּתָאִים

פִּיהֶם לְמַלְקוֹשׁ עֲנָנִי

נָטַף בְּשָׂמִי עֲלֵיהֶם

בְּשֶׁם עֲנַן קִנְּמוֹנִי

One keeps on saying, "Kind sir,"

    while inside, he's scheming to get you.

Their fathers were people so vile

    I wouldn't have them as sheepdogs!

They can't even blush without smearing

    their faces all over with rouge!

They seem to themselves to be giants—

    to me they're no bigger than crickets.

When I start to declaim a poem,

    they gripe, as if it were Greek:

"Speak in a language we know!

    This is just Ashkelon babble!"

Watch me tread them like mud,

    for I have a tongue like a pitchfork.

Why am I ringing my bell?—

    Your ears are just covered with foreskin!

Your necks are too scrawny to bear

    the golden adornments I fashion.

Why don't those idiots open

    their mouths to the rain of my clouds;

my fragrance would drip down upon them—

    the cinnamon scent of my clouds.

אוֹי לַתְּבוּנָה וְאוֹי לִי

כִּי גוֹי כְּמוֹ זֶה שְׁכֵנִי

דַּעַת אֱלֹהִים יְשִׁימוּן

כְּאוֹב וְכַיִּדְעֹנִי

עַל זֹאת אֱיֵלִיל וְאֶסְפֹּד

אָשִׁית בְּמוֹ שַׂק מְלוֹנִי

אָכֹף כְּאַגְמֹן וְאָצוּם

שֵׁנִי חֲמִישִׁי וְשֵׁנִי

מַה־זֶּה אֲיַחֵל אֲנִי עוֹד

אוֹ מַה־יְּהִי בִטְחוֹנִי

עֵינַי בְּתֵבֵל תְּשׁוֹטֵט

לֹא תֶחֱזֶה־בָּהּ רְצוֹנִי

תִּיקַר תְּמוּתָהּ בְּעֵינַי

תֵּקַל אֲדָמָה בְּאָזְנִי

אִם יֵשְׁטְ לִבִּי לְדַרְכָּהּ

לִטְמוֹן בְּחָבִּי עֲוֹנִי

יֵשֵׁב עֲמָלִי בְרֹאשִׁי

יֵרֵד בְּחֵיקִי זְדֹנִי

נַפְשִׁי כְּבוֹדָהּ תְּמָאֵן

כִּי עִם כְּבוֹדָהּ קְלוֹנִי

לֹא אֶעֱלָז־בָּהּ לְעוֹלָם

לֹא יַעֲלָז־בָּהּ גְּאוֹנִי

Woe for wisdom and me

    that I'm stuck with men as my neighbors

who think of Knowledge of God

    as necromancy or witchcraft!

That's why I wail and lament,

    spend the night huddled in sackcloth,

bent like a reed, fasting Mondays,

    Thursdays, and Mondays again.

Why should I keep on hoping?

    Where can I place my trust?

I roam the world with my eye

    and find what I'm seeking—nowhere.

Death seems dear to my eyes;

    the world means little to me.

If I should ever pursue the world

    (harboring sin in my core),

may punishment fall on my head,

    may my crime devolve upon me!

My soul spurns the world's honors.

    Honors like those would be shame.

I cannot rejoice in it ever,

    my pride could never enjoy it,

לוּ קָרְאוּ לִי בְּנֵי עָשׁ

סוּרָה שְׁבָה־פֹּה פְּלֹנִי

כִּי הָיְתָה הָאֲדָמָה

כָּעֹל עֲלֵי צַוָּרְנִי

מַה־לִּי אֲנִי עוֹד בְּתֵבֵל

לוּלֵי שְׂאֵת עֶוְרוֹנִי

נַפְשִׁי בְּמוֹתִי תְרַנֵּן

לוּ מָצְאָה צוּר מְעוֹנִי

אָקֵץ בְּחַיַּי וְאֶמְאַס

לִהְיוֹת בְּשָׂרִי מְכוֹנִי

כִּי יוֹם שְׂשׂוֹנִי אֲסוֹנִי

וּבְיוֹם אֲסוֹנִי שְׂשׂוֹנִי

אִיגַע לְהָבִין וְאֵדַע

כִּכְלוֹת בְּשָׂרִי וְאוֹנִי

כִּי סוֹף אֲנָחָה הֲנָחָה

וְעֵקֶב רְזוֹנִי מְזוֹנִי

אֶדְרֹשׁ בְּעוֹדִי אֲחַפֵּשׂ

כְּמִצְוַת שְׁלֹמֹה זְקֵנִי

אוּלַי מְגַלֶּה עֲמֻקּוֹת

יְגַלֶּה תְבוּנָה לְעֵינִי

כִּי הִיא מְנָתִי לְבַדָּהּ

מִכָּל־עֲמָלִי וְאוֹנִי.

even if I were offered a place

     by the side of the Bear and his sons.

Yes, the world has turned out to be

     a yoke that weighs down my neck.

Why am I in it at all,

     except to bear my own blindness?

My soul would be happy to die,

     if it found a home with the Lord.

I hate my life. I refuse

     to treat this flesh as my home,

for the day of my doom is my joy,

     and the day of my joy is my doom.

I labor to learn, and I find

     as my flesh and my strength give way,

that sorrows are followed by comfort,

     and famine is followed by fullness.

While I live, I will carry on seeking,

     as my ancestor Solomon bade me.

Perhaps the Revealer of mysteries,

     will reveal to me some of His wisdom.

That, at least, is what's due me

     in exchange for all I have suffered.

רְבִיבֵי דְמָעֵךְ הָיוּ רְסִיסִים

וְהָיוּ כַּבְּקָעוֹת הָרְכָסִים

וְאֵיכָה לֹא תְזַמֵּר הַזְּמוֹרָה

וְלָמָּה לֹא תְהַלֵּל הָעֲסִיסִים

אֲשֶׁר רָדְפוּ יְגוֹנֶיךָ וְנָסוּ

מְנַסַּת בֶּן־נְבָט אֶל תַּחְפְּנֵסִים

עֲנִיתִיו הַלְּבָבוֹת שֶׁכְחוּ רִישׁ

וְשָׂמְחוּ בָם כְּשִׂמְחָה בַּנְּכָסִים

וְגַם שָׁטוּ וְעָטוּ בַּתְּלָאוֹת

וְהָיוּ עַל כְּנַף רוּחַ עֲמָסִים

בְּנֵיהֶם עָזְבוּ בַבַּר כְּעֹרֵב

וְיַלְדֵיהֶם הֱנִיסוּם כַּפְּרָסִים

וְלֹא הָיָה גְבִיעֵנוּ כְּיַם סוּף

עֲדֵי הָיוּ יְגוֹנֵינוּ חֲנֵסִים

וְאוּלָם הֶעֱלָה קָצִיר סְפִיחִים

וְגַם עָשׂוּ סְפִיחֵיהֶם שְׁחִיסִים

וְהִנֵּה הֶחֳלִי בִּלָּה בְשָׂרִי

וְשָׁם בִּשְׂאָר שְׁאֵרִי אֵשׁ הֲמָסִים

"YOUR TEARS, which were a downpour, now are droplets,
      and mountains once impassable are plains.
Then why not praise the vine in verse
      and sing a paean to the wine
that puts your woe to flight like Jeroboam
      fleeing Solomon to Egypt?"

But I replied:
      Hearts can forget their poverty.
      They almost like the grape as much as wealth.
It sets their troubles wandering, flying off,
      as if on wings of wind,
abandoning their children in the wilderness, like ravens;
      chasing away their young, like vultures.
I, too, once had a goblet. It was my Red Sea,
      my sorrows its Egyptians.
But sorrow's harvest bred an aftergrowth,
      from which a secondary aftergrowth has sprung,
and now my flesh is wasted with disease,
      and what is left is burning fit to melt—

עֲדֵי הָיוּ נִזְמֵינוּ עֲטָרוֹת

וְהָיוּ טַבְּעֹתֵינוּ עֲכָסִים

וּבָעֵר הַקְּרָבִים עַל יְקוֹד אֵשׁ

וְדִמִּינוּ עֲצָמֵינוּ נְמֵסִים

קְרָבִים שֻׁלְּחוּ בָהֶם חֲלָיִים

וּמִצְוַת הַזְּמָן שֹׁמְרִים וְעֹשִׂים

וְאֵיךְ לֹא יִהְיוּ אֶפֶס וָתֹהוּ

עֲצָמוֹת בַּתְּלָאוֹת הֵם אֲבוּסִים

חֲמָסִי עַל חֲלִי כִּלָּה שְׁאֵרִי

וְשָׁם אַלּוֹן בְּעֵינֵי עֵין הֲדַסִּים

וְעַל הַלַּיְלָה אָשִׁית חֲמָסִי

אֲשֶׁר שָׁת אָהֳלֵי חֹשֶׁךְ פְּרֻשִׂים

וְאֶהְגֶּה־בָּם כְּיוֹנִים וַאֲצַפְצֵף

בְּשִׂיחִי כַּעֲגוּרִים אוֹ כְסִיסִים

וְלֹא תִרְאֶה שְׁחָקִים יִשְׁלְחוּ שַׁי

וְיוֹבִילוּן לְעַפְעַפַּי שְׁבִיסִים

וְעַפְעַפַּי בְּהַבִּיטִי אֲלֵיהֶם

כְּלָאוֹת וְהֵמָּה כַּקְּרָסִים

שְׁמַרְתִּים בֶּאֱמוּנָתִי כְּאִלּוּ

אֲנִי רֹעֶה וְהֵמָּה הַכְּבָשִׂים

חֲשַׁבְתִּימוֹ אֲחֵי בָרָק וְהִנֵּה

בְּאָחוֹר שֻׁבְּחוּ רוּחָם כְּסוּסִים

a signet ring could serve me for a crown,

    an earring for an anklet.

My guts are roasting on a grill,

    I seem to feel my members melting—

guts to which diseases have been sent by Time,

    and they obey Time's will.

What can bones do but disintegrate,

    when all they've had to batten on was trouble?

I rage against this flesh-consuming illness

    that makes mere myrtles seem like oaks to me.

Then, too, I rage against the night,

    the night that pitches tents of darkness

under which I moan like doves, I screech, complain

    like flocks of cranes or swallows.

You do not see the skies bestowing gifts,

    or bringing ornaments to deck my eyes,

but when I gaze at them all through the night,

    it seems as if my eyes are loops and they are hooks.

I watch them like a faithful shepherd,

    they my sheep.

I used to think them lightning-swift, but now

    they seem to hold their spirit back, like jaded horses.

וְדִמִּיתִים מְיֻדָּעֵי עֲשָׂהאֵל

וְהִנֵּה הֵם אֲחֵי פִּסְחֵי יְבוּסִים

בְּאָמְרִי מַה־לְּבוּשׁ קָדִים יְשִׁיבוּן

תְּכֵלֶת וַעֲלוֹת שַׁחַר מְכַסִּים

וְעֵת כִּי הֶעֱלָה שַׁחַר דְּגָלָיו

וְהֵרִים כּוֹכְבֵי בֹקֶר כָּנֵסִים

קְרָבַי שָׁקְטוּ כִּי נִמְלְאוּ טָל

וְעָלַי נִגְּרוּ נִטְפֵי רְסִיסִים.

I thought that they were fleet as Asael;

    they turn out to be lame as Jebusites.

When I ask, "What garment wears the East?"

    they answer, "Dawn is dressed in violet."

But when at last the dawn lifts up its banners,

    raises the morning stars aloft like flags,

my insides, filled with dew, at last subside,

    as gentle drops of grace drip over me.

הֲלֹא אֲצַדֵּק בְּאָמְרִי כִּי אֲמָרָיו

כְּגִשְׁמֵי עָב אֲשֶׁר עַל גֵּז הֲרִיקָם

סְפוֹת חֶסֶד עֲלֵי חֶסֶד בְּשָׁפְטוֹ

כְּמִשְׁפָּט שֹׁמְרֵי חֶסֶד וְחָקָם

וּמַה־יַּמְרִיץ מְחֹקֵק בָּאֱנוֹשׁ לוֹ

יְהִי צַוָּאר אֱנוֹשׁ הָיָה עֲנָקָם

וּמַה־יֹּאמַר לְרֵעֵהוּ אֱנוֹשׁ לוֹ

קְרָאוּ מֵעֲפַר אֶרֶץ אֲזִי קָם

וְאוּלָם כָּלְאוּ רַגְלֵי נְגָעִים

בְּגֵוִי יַעֲשׂוּ כָלָה וְנָקָם

אֲשֶׁר אִם אָמְרָה יִכְלוּן יְנוּבוּן

וְיַעַל מִבְּשָׂרֵי אֵד וְהִשְׁקָם

כְּאִלּוּ הֶעֱלָם גַּבֵּי בְחָנֵס

לְמוּל פִּיחִים אֲשֶׁר מֹשֶׁה זְרָקָם

חֲמָתָם כַּחֲמַת עַכְשׁוּב וְתַנִּין

וְאֶחְשֹׁב כִּי אֲבִיר נָקָם נְשָׁקָם

I KNOW I'M right in likening his words
      to rain that clouds have sprinkled on cut grass,
in saying that his judgments join
      benevolence and charity,
      as is the way of every man of generosity.
But what is gained when poets lavish words
      upon a man who could be called
      an ornament to mankind's throat?
What answer can a man make to a friend
      for whom he'd rise up from the sepulchre
      to serve, if summoned?
The problem is my legs: immobilized by pustules
      that wreak revenge and ruin on my body.
Just when I think they're cured, they flourish,
      watered by a mist that rises from my flesh,
rising on my back as when in Egypt
      Moses flung soot in handfuls skyward.
Their venom sizzles like a snake's or viper's,
      as if stoked by a vengeful deity.

וְאַל תִּתְמַהּ לְכָל־אֵלֶּה תְּמַהּ כִּי

בְּאֵין עֵצִים וָאֵשׁ יֹאפוּ בְצֵקָם

וְעוֹרֵיהֶם כְּמוֹ עוֹרֵי יְרִיעוֹת

אֲרַגָּם בֶּן־אֲחִיסָמָךְ וְרָקָם

אֲשֶׁר יִתְרֹצְצוּ בָנִים בְּקִרְבָּם

עֲדֵי הַלַּיְלָה דָּמֵי הֲנִיקָם

וְלוּ רָאָם רְאֵם יָשׁוּב וְחָשַׁב

גְּאוֹן יַרְדֵּן לְפִיהוּ לֹא יְרָקָם

וְיִדְמוּ בַּהֲמוֹת לִבָּם לְהֹרוֹת

אֲשֶׁר הַצַּר וְהַצִּיר הֶחֱזִיקָם

כְּשׁוֹשַׁנִּים נְשָׂאוּם לְקֹטֵיהֶם

עֲדֵי כִי כָרְתוּ שׁוֹקָם בְּשׁוֹקָם

וְיַזְכִּירוּן לְבָבִי נַחֲלֵי נֹף

אֲשֶׁר הָיוּ לְדָם בְּרֹאוֹת אֲפִיקָם

וְהָעֵת יִפְעֲרוּ פִיהֶם יְשִׁימוֹן

לְבוּשֵׁי חוּר וְאַרְגָּמָן בְּרִקְמָם

כְּמוֹ דֶרֶךְ אֱוִיל דַּרְכָּם וְאִלּוּ

אֱוִיל שָׁמָם בְּמַכְתֵּשׁ לֹא שְׁחָקָם

וְהָעֵת יִדְרְכֵם אִישׁ יִתְּנוּ קוֹל

כְּשֵׁמַע קוֹל שְׂפָתַיִם בְּנָשְׁקָם

כְּאִלּוּ נַעֲשׂוּ בִּידֵי בְצַלְאֵל

וּבִשְׁתֵּי כִכְּרֵי כֶסֶף יְצָקָם

But don't let that surprise you. Here's the wonder:

    they bake my skin like dough but don't use wood or fire!

They have a membrane like the leather curtains

    that Oholiav fashioned for the Tabernacle.

Inside are fetuses that push and shove,

    until the night gives them my blood to suck.

Seeing them, the River Beast would quite forget

    he'd ever swallowed Jordan's rushing waters.

Their insides sometimes throb like pregnant women

    seized by agonizing birth pangs.

They look like roses carried off by gatherers

    with legs all scratched and bloody from the stalks.

Their flux puts me in mind of Egypt's rivers

    turned to blood by Moses' miracle.

When their mouths gape wide, they dye

    my clothing white and purple with their ooze.

Like nitwits: you can put them in a mortar,

    but you'll never crush them with a pestle.

When a person squeezes them, they make a sound

    like lips being kissed.

Bezalel might have fashioned them,

    casting each one from a silver ingot.

וְהָאֶחָד קְרָאתִיו בֶּן־נְתַנְיָה
וְהַשֵּׁנִי גְּדַלְיָה בֶּן־אֲחִיקָם
וְהָיִינוּ תְמוֹל רָצִים כְּסוּסִים
יְכַסֶּה אֶת־פְּאַת שַׁחַק אֲבָקָם
וְהַיּוֹם כֻּשְׁלוּ בִרְכַּי וְנֶעְלַם
מְקוֹמָם מִמְּךָ אָחִי וּפִיקָם

וְשָׁלַחְתִּי לְךָ שִׂיחִי בְּיַד צִיר
לְבַל יָשׁוּב לְךָ נָעוּר וְרֵיקָם
עֲדֵי אָשִׁית חֲסָדֶיךָ לְנֶגְדִּי
וְשִׁלַּמְתִּי אֲזַי חָקָם לְחֵיקָם.

I've named the one Ishmael ben Netaniah,
        Gedaliah ben Ahikam is the other.
There was a time when I ran like a stallion,
        blanketing the horizon with my dust,
but now my knees have failed. That's why
        you do not see them or their stumbling, friend.

I've sent these verses by your messenger,
        so that he not return with empty hands,
against the day my eyes behold your grace.
        Then I'll requite your kindnesses in kind.

אֲהָהּ לִי מִזְּמַן מֵנִיר יְחִידִים
וְהָהּ לִי מִנֻּדָּד עַכַּר יְדִידִים
הֲלֹא הֵם הֶחֱרִידוּ רַעְיוֹנִי
וְהִשְׁמִיעוּ לְאָזְנִי קוֹל פְּחָדִים
וְלִבִּי לְהֲטוּ מֵאֵשׁ וְנָתְנוּ
עֲלֵי עֵינִי לְבַל אִישַׁן פְּקִידִים
וְאֵיךְ אִישַׁן וְעַפְעַפַּי קְשֻׁרִים
בְּגַבּוֹתַי וְאִישׁוֹנִי עֲקֻדִים
וְדִמְעוֹתַי בְּתוֹךְ עֵינַי מְחַכִּים
הֲמוֹת לִבִּי כְּחַכֵּי אִישׁ גְּדוּדִים
וְכִסּוּ עֲנָנֵיהֶם עַל מְאוֹרָם
עֲדֵי הֵם מֵרְאוֹת דּוֹדִי כְּבֵדִים
וּמֵאָז הַיְגוֹנִים נִלְחֲמוּ בָם
וְיָדָם אָחֲזָה חֶרֶב נְדֻדִים
יְנוּסוּן מֵאֲשׁוּנֵי נֶחְשָׁלִים
לְעַפְעַפַּי וְהֵם נָעִים וְנָדִים
וְיַעַל מִצְּלָעַי אֵשׁ וְלֹא אֶ –
כְּלוֹ רַק יֶעְשָׁנוּ עֵינַי כְּאוּדִים
וְכִמְעַט יַאֲבִידוּ אֶת-לְבָבִי
וְלֹא יֵדְעוּ הֲכִי הֵם מַאֲבִידִים
אֲבָל כִּי מָעֲדוּ רַגְלַי וְלֹא אֶ –
רָאֶה חַח וְהִנָּם בַּמְּצוֹדִים

POOR ME! Time drives away the best of men.

    Alas! How separation ruins friendships.

These two put terror in my mind

    and strike my ear with panic,

inflame my heart and post a watch

    upon my eyes so that I cannot sleep.

How could I sleep? My eyes are fastened

    to my brow, the lids lashed open.

Tears lurk in my eyes, like troops in ambush,

    waiting for my heart to surge.

They shade my eyes with tear-clouds, hide the light,

    my eyes are dim, I cannot see my friends.

Sorrows long ago have taken up

    the sword of banishment and made war on my tears,

since which, they stream, spent warriors, from my eyes,

    always on the move, and always running.

Fire rises from my ribs, but they are not consumed;

    my eyes smoke, smoldering like half-burned brands.

(They nearly make a ruin of my heart,

    though not aware that they're its ruination.)

And since I cannot see the thorns, I trip,

    and suddenly my feet are in a trap!

לְפֵרוּדְךָ יְדִיד נַפְשִׁי שְׁמוּאֵל

אֲנִי נִבְהָל וְרַעְיוֹנַי חֲרֵדִים

לְמַעַן יוֹם נְדֹד נִשְׁאַר לְבָבִי

וְהָיָה עִם לְבָבְךָ לַאֲחָדִים

בְּלִי נֹדְךָ אֲנִי עֶבֶד לְיָמִים

וּבְנָדְדְךָ אֲנִי עֶבֶד עֲבָדִים

אֲהָהּ כִּי רְדָפוּנִי הַתְּלָאוֹת

וְהָיִינוּ לְעֵין יָמִים שְׁדוּדִים

בְּזֹיתִים וַאֲנִי שָׁלֵו בְּבֵיתִי

וְהֵם הָיוּ לְהַנָּקֵם עֲתִידִים

וְהָיוּ מִתְּמוֹל שֹׁגִים וְהַיּוֹם

לְהָרְגֵנִי בְעָרְמָה הֵם מְזִידִים

לְזֹאת אֶשֹּׁם וְיִשְׁתּוֹמֵם לְבָבִי

וְשָׂבַעְתִּי עֲדֵי נֶשֶׁף נְדֻדִים

וְאוֹחִיל עַד עֲלוֹת שַׁחַר לְדוֹדִים

וְנִתְעַנַּג וְנִתְעַלֵּס בְּדוֹדִים

וְגֵרִים גֹּרְשׁוּ מִבֵּית מְכוֹנָם

אֱלֹהִים יַעֲשֶׂה לָהֶם מְצָדִים

וּבֵית הָאַהֲבָה יִבְנֶה וְתוֹכוֹ

מְנוּחָה יִמְצְאוּ רַגְלֵי מְנָדִים

וְיַנְחֵם אֶל מְחוֹז חֶפְצָם וְיָמִיר

בְּקוֹל שָׂשׂוֹן וְשִׂמְחָה קוֹל פְּחָדִים.

With you away, my soul-friend Samuel,

    I live in horror, with my mind in terror,

for when you part, my heart,

    a part of yours, remains behind.

When you are here, I am a slave to Time,

    but with you gone, I'm just a slave of slaves.

Poor me, with hardships always at my back,

    as if attacked by highwaymen in daylight!

Content at home, I felt contempt for them,

    but they were bound to get revenge.

Once they were unwitting, but today

    they plot to kill me with design.

I'm shaken. My heart knows horror.

    My vigils last until first morning's light.

I wait for dawn, when I can see my friends,

    so that we can take our pleasure

    and enjoy companionship.

As for strangers, turned out from their homes,

    may God provide them fortresses secure

and build a chamber there for love,

    where exiles' feet can get some rest,

and may He guide them to the longed-for goal,

    exchange the sounds of fear for sounds of joy.

הֲלֹא גֹדֶל חֶלִי גִּדַּל יְגוֹנִי

וְכֹחִי מֵחֲמָתוֹ סָר וְאוֹנִי

וְהָעֵת שֶׁקְּרָאַנִי כְתָבְךָ

בְּגֹדֶל נֹעֲמוֹ הִשְׁקִיט שְׁאוֹנִי

וְלֹא אֶכְתֹּב לְהוֹדִיעַ בְּחָלְיִי

אֲבָל אֶכְתֹּב לְכַפֵּר אֶת־עֲוֹנִי

לְמַעַן לֹא דְרַשְׁתִּיךָ וְאוּלָם

אֲנִי אֵלֵךְ עֲלֵי פָנַי וְעֵינִי

וְאֵדַע כִּי בְּעֵת אָשׁוּר דְּמוּתְךָ

אֲזַי אֶרֶף וְיָסוּר דַּאֲבוֹנִי.

I'M AILING, I'm in misery
  with fever that has drained my energy.
I read your message, and it did me good,
  alleviated my anxiety.
I'm writing not to tell you my condition,
  rather to atone for my transgression
in failing to attend you. One day soon,
  you'll see me walking on my face and eyes.
I know that once I get a glimpse of you,
  I will be healed, my body good as new.

מִשְׁמַן בְּשָׂרִי יִדַּל

וּכְאֵב לְבָבִי יִגְדַּל

בְּקֶרֶב תְּפִלַּת מִנְחָה

וַאֲנִי לְבַדִּי נִבְדָּל

לֹא אֶשְׁמְעָה זֶה כַּמָּה

שַׁדַּי וְלֹא יִתְגַּדָּל

אֶזְכֹּר עֲלוֹתִי אֶל בֵּית

אֵל יוֹם וְיוֹם לֹא אֶחְדָּל

שָׁבְתִּי חֲצוֹת הַיּוֹם שָׁם

לִזְכֹּר לְשֵׁם אֶלֶף דָּל

תַּחַת כְּנָפְךָ אֶחְסֶה

מַחְסֶה וּמָעוֹז לַדַּל

הַצֵּל לְדַל וּפְתַח דַּל

עֲטֹף כְּדַל מִבּוֹר דָּל.

MY FLESH is wasting,

    my heartache waxing.

It's afternoon, and time for Minḥah prayers,

    and here I am, alone.

How long since last I heard

    God's Name or Kaddish said!

I remember going every day

    to the house of God,

spending midday there,

    pronouncing "Adonai," His Name.

O shelter, fortress of the lowly,

    here I huddle, underneath your wing,

in need, emaciated, in the pit—

    raise me, save me, lend me voice!

בְּשָׂרִי דַל מְאֹד מֵרֹב דְּאָגָה
וְאִם אֵשֵׁב בְּעַיִן יָשֵׁן הַיַּחַ
וְחֹתָמִי אֲשֶׁר הָיָה בְּיָדִי
אֲנִי חֹגֵר לְמַחְגֹּרֶת וּמֵזַח.

CARES HAVE turned me scrawny. You could throw me
    into the eye of someone sound asleep—I'd not be felt.
The ring that once was snug around my finger
    I wear around my waist now, as a belt.

אִם תֶּאֱהַב לִהְיוֹת בְּאַנְשֵׁי חָלֶד
אִם נַפְשְׁךָ תָגוּר שְׁבִיבֵי פָלֶד
הָקֵל יְקָר תֵּבֵל וְאַל יַשִּׁיאָךְ
עשֶׁר וְלֹא כָבוֹד וְגַם לֹא יָלֶד
יֵקַל בְּעֵינֶיךָ מְאֹד קָלוֹן וָרֵישׁ
מוֹת מִבְּלִי בֵן כַּאֲשֶׁר מֵת סָלֶד
דַּע נַפְשְׁךָ הֵיטֵב בְּיַעַן הִיא לְבַד
מִן הַשְּׁאָר נִשְׁאָר וּמִן הַגֹּלֶד.

IF YOU DESIRE to live eternal life,

> and if you live in fear of flames eternal,

make light of worldly rank; don't be beguiled

> by honors, wealth, or progeny.

Make light of shame and poverty;

> die without a son, like Seled.

But learn to know your soul, and know it well,

> for it alone survives the flesh and skin.

וְלֵב נָבוּב וְתוּשִׁיָּה סְתוּמָה

וְגוּף נִרְאָה וְנֶפֶשׁ נַעֲלָמָה

וְאֶרֶץ שֶׁחֲרֶיהָ יִמְצְאוּ רָע

וְלֹא שָׂשׂוֹן לְאָדָם בָּאֲדָמָה

וְעֶבֶד יַהֲרֹג הַיּוֹם אֲדֹנָיו

וְשִׁפְחָה יִסְרָה מַלְכָּה וְאָמָה

וּבֵן יָקוּם עֲלֵי אָבִיו וְאִמּוֹ

וְכֵן הַבַּת בְּאָבִיהָ וְאִמָּהּ

יְדִידִי רָאֲתָה עֵינִי בְּתֵבֵל

אֲשֶׁר הַטּוֹב בְּעֵינֵי כֹל מְהוּמָה

יְמֵי חַיֵּי אֱנוֹשׁ יִשָּׂא עֲמָלִים

וְיִשָּׂא אַחֲרִיתוֹ גּוּשׁ וְרִמָּה

וְתָשׁב הָאֲדָמָה לָאֲדָמָה

וְתַעַל הַנְּשָׁמָה לַנְּשָׁמָה.

THE MIND is flawed, the way to wisdom blocked.

> The flesh alone is seen, the soul is hidden.

Men who seek the world find only evil.

> A man can get no pleasure here on earth.

The servant rises up and kills his lord.

> Serving girls attack their mistresses.

Sons rise up to strike their parents, even girls

> lift hands in violence against their elders.

My friend, from what I've seen of life, I'd say

> the best that you can hope is to go mad.

However long you live, you suffer toil,

> and in the end, you suffer worms and rot,

until the day when clay goes back to clay;

> until the soul ascends to join the Soul.

אִם אַחֲרִית שִׂמְחַת אֲדָמָה אֵבֶל

גַּם סוֹף מְנוּחָתָהּ לְטִיט וַחֵבֶל

וִימֵי אֱנוֹשׁ כַּצֵּל אֲשֶׁר לֹא יַעֲמֹד

פִּתְאֹם יְהִי נִשְׁבָּר כְּשֶׁבֶר נֵבֶל

עַל מַה־נְּבַקֵּשׁ בִּלְעֲדֵי שַׁדַּי הֲלֹא

כָּל־מַעֲשֵׂינוּ בִּלְעֲדֵי זֹאת הָבֶל.

SINCE ALL LIFE'S joys are doomed to end in sorrow,
    and all life's pleasures end in dirt and pain;
since all man's days are nothing but a shadow,
    and man is destined to be smashed like pottery,
why should we seek anything but God?
    Nothing else in life is worth the doing.

Patrons, Friends,
and Enemies

אֲנִי כָל־אוֹהֲבַי אֵהַב בְּכָל־לֵב
וְגַם לִמְכַבְּדַי תָּמִיד אֲכַבֵּד
וְלִי לָשׁוֹן כְּעֵט סוֹפֵר יְשַׁנֵּן
שֶׁבַח רֵעַי וְכָל־קָמַי יְאַבֵּד.

I'M LOYAL to my friends with all my heart.
  I always honor those who honor me.
My tongue is sharp as any court scribe's pen
    to praise a friend, to crush an enemy.

מִי זֹאת כְּמוֹ שַׁחַר עָלָה וְנִשְׁקָפָה

תָּאִיר כְּמוֹ חַמָּה בָּרָה מְאֹד יָפָה

כְּבוּדָה כְּבַת מֶלֶךְ עֲדִינָה מְעֻנָּגָה

רֵיחָהּ כְּרֵיחַ מֹר מֻקְטָר וְכִשְׂרֵפָה

לְחִיָּהּ כְּשׁוֹשַׁנָּה בַּדָּם מְאָדֶּמֶת

אֶרְאֶה כְשָׁפִים בָּהּ וְאֵינָה מְכַשֵּׁפָה

תַּעְדֶּה עֲדִי זָהָב וּמִינֵי בְדָלְחִים

וּבְכָל־יְקָר אֶבֶן סַפִּיר מְעֻלָּפָה

כְּסַהַר בְּמוֹלָדוֹ כְּתָרָהּ עֲלֵי רֹאשָׁהּ

שֶׁהִיא מְשַׂהֶמֶת כָּלָּה מְיֻשָּׁפָה

כִּי נִרְאֲתָה לִי מֵרָחוֹק חֲשַׁבְתִּיהָ

יוֹנָה תְּדַלֵּג עַל שָׂדֶה וְהִיא עָפָה

רַצְתִּי לְקָרְבָתָהּ עֵת שֶׁרְאִיתִיהָ

עֵת רָאֲתָה אֹתִי אָז כִּסְּתָה אַפָּהּ

אָנָה פְּנוֹתֵךְ אָן וְהַיּוֹם מְאֹד פָּנָה

וְתֵבֵל רְאִי לוּלֵי אוֹרֵךְ כְּמוֹ עֵיפָה

תָּנִיד שְׂפָתֶיהָ אָז לַהֲשִׁיבֵנִי

כְּאִלּוּ מְרִיקָה צוּף בָּהֶם וּמַטִּיפָה

לִרְאוֹת שְׁמוּאֵל הָרֹאֶה אֲנִי עֹלָה

לִהְיוֹת לְבֵיתוֹ סֹבֶבֶת וּמַקִּיפָה

WHO IS THIS rising like the dawn? Who peers
  sunlike, clear and beautiful,
dignified and delicate as royalty,
  fragrant as if censed with myrrh and incense,
her cheek a rose, blood-tinted,
  bewitching me (though surely no witch, she!),
bedecked with gold and crystal,
  studded with precious gems,
and on her head, a diadem—a sickle moon—
  set all around with beryls and with jaspers?
From far away, she might have been a dove,
  hopping, fluttering about a field.
I saw her, and I hurried to her side.
  She saw me, and she covered up her face.
"Where to, my lady? Day is nearly gone,
  there's no more light except what comes from you."
She moved her lips to answer, and it seemed
  that she was dripping honey as she spoke:
"I'm off to visit Samuel the Seer,
  to circumambulate his house in reverence."

וְאָז עֲנִיתִיהָ אַל תֵּלְכִי אַל כִּי

אֹתוֹ בְּחַיָּתֵךְ לֹא תִהְיִי צֹפָה

כִּי מֵת וְגַם יָרַד לִשְׁאוֹל בְּרָב־חֵשֶׁק

כָּלָה בְּאַהֲבָתוֹ אֹתָךְ וְגַם נִסְפָּה

לְכִי אֶל שְׁמוּאֵל שֶׁעָלָה בְּאַרְצֵנוּ

כַּעֲלוֹת שְׁמוּאֵל בָּרָמָה וּבַמִּצְפָּה

חֲקֹר תְּבוּנָה שֶׁכָּל סוֹד סְתָרֶיהָ

גִּלָּה וְנִפְזֶרֶת שָׁמָּה מְאַסָּפָה

שְׁלַל שְׁלָלֶיהָ וְכָמַס בְּאֹצְרוֹתָיו

וּבָטַח בְּמַחְמַדֵּי זְהָבָהּ וְגַם כַּסְפָּהּ

דּוֹדִי יְדִיד נַפְשִׁי אַתָּה צְרִי מַכְאוֹב

וּלְכָל־חֳלִי אַתְּ כַּתְּעָלָה וְכַתְּרוּפָה

לִמְאֹד אֲהַבְתִּיךָ אֵין קֵץ לְאַהֲבָתָךְ

הִנְנִי בְחָנֵנִי וְלִבִּי בְּזֹאת צָרְפָה

וּמֵאַהֲבָתִי בָךְ שִׁירִי יְהוֹדֶךָ

יַרְבָּה דְבַר צַחוֹת לֹא לַעֲגֵי שָׂפָה

כָּל־בַּעֲלֵי הַשִּׁיר חָרְדוּ לְעֻמָּתוֹ

אַף יָעַטוּ בֹשֶׁת כֻּלָּם וְגַם חֶרְפָּה.

I said, "Don't bother going, there's no point,
 for never will you see him while you live.
He has died—he died for love of you—
 was swept away, descended to Sheol.
Go see our land's new Samuel, now arisen,
 as Samuel the Seer arose of old
 in Ramah and Mizpah.
He searched out wisdom and its mysteries,
 assembled all its strewn and scattered bits,
swept up its booty, stowed them with his treasures,
 put his trust in their delights,
 not in gold and silver."

Dear friend, you are the balm for every pain,
 the remedy, the universal cure.
My love for you is great—no, endless.
 Here I am: Just put me to the test.
My loving song will praise you eloquently,
 correctly, not in garbled speech.
Verse-writing men will tremble in its presence,
 cowering in shame and obloquy.

וְאַתְּ יוֹנָה חֲבַצֶּלֶת שָׁרוֹנִים

וְשׁוּלַיִךְ מְלֵאִים פַּעֲמוֹנִים

וְרִמֹּנֵי מְעִילַיִךְ זְהוּבִים

אֲשֶׁר יִדְמוּ מְעִילֵי אַהֲרֹנִים

וְעֵת צֵאתֵךְ לְעָמְתִי אֲדָמָּה

הֲלִיכָתֵךְ כְּשֶׁמֶשׁ בַּמְּעוֹנִים

שְׁבִי פֹה יַעֲלַת הַחֵן לְנֶגְדִּי

וְהָעִירִי לְדוֹדֵךְ הַשְּׁשׁוֹנִים

קְחִי הַתֹּף וְהַנֵּבֶל וְשִׁירִי

בְּנִגּוּנֵךְ עֲלֵי עָשׂוֹר וּמִנִּים

וְקוּמִי הַלֲלִי דוֹדֵךְ בְּחִירֵךְ

יְקוּתִיאֵל נְשִׂיא שָׂרִים וְרֹזְנִים

מְאוֹר עוֹלָם יְסוֹד אַדְנֵי מְכוֹנָיו

וְעַמּוּדֵי מְרוֹמִים בּוֹ נְכוֹנִים

אֲשֶׁר כָּל־רֹזְנִים אֵלָיו מְיַחֲלִים

וְלִדְבָרוֹ מְקַוִּים כָּל־סְגָנִים

אֲשֶׁר יִדְרֹשׁ עֲדֵי יִיגַע בְּחֶפְצָם

כְּאָב יִדְרֹשׁ מְצֹא טֶרֶף לְבָנִים

אֲשֶׁר פִּיהוּ לְכָל־אָדָם בְּשׂוֹרָה

וְנִדְבָתוֹ יְקָרָה מִפְּנִינִים

AH, DOVE, you Sharon rose
>with skirts all hung with bells,

all hung with golden pomegranates
>like the robes of priests:

As you come my way, you seem to rise
>like the very sun in heaven.

Sit here by me, O loveliest gazelle,
>and stir your lover's pleasure.

Take up the drum and lute; accompany
>your singing with a ten-stringed harp.

Rise and praise your love, your favorite,
>Yekutiel, the lord of potentates,

illumination of the world, the world's foundation,
>the man on whom the pillars of the heavens rest secure.

Rulers repose their hopes in him,
>and courtiers hang upon his every word.

He works to weariness on their behalf,
>the way a father works to feed his children.

He has a kindly word for every man—
>and then there are his gifts, worth more than pearls!

בְּרוּחוֹ חֵן וּבְלְבָבוֹ נְדָבָה

וְשִׂפְתוֹתָיו בְּכָל־עֵת נֶאֱמָנִים

גְּבִיר דּוֹמֶה כְּשַׂחַק עַל אֲדָמָה

וְגַם כַּפָּיו לְהַמְטִיר כַּעֲנָנִים

בְּהֶעָצְרָם יְמוּתוּן הַנְּפָשׁוֹת

וְיִמָּלְאוּן בְּהַמְטִירָם רְנָנִים

יְמַלֵּא אֵל מְהֵרָה מִשְׁאֲלוֹתָיו

וְיִהְיוּ מִשְׁאֲלוֹתַי לוֹ נְתָנִים.

His spirit is benign, his heart is liberal,

> his lips trustworthy ever.

A lord, a veritable sky above the earth,

> with hands like clouds for bounty:

When they dry up, the people perish,

> but when they pour, they fill the folk with song.

May God fulfill his wishes speedily,

> and may my wishes be consigned to him!

כָּל־הַזְּמַנִּים מִימֵי קֶדֶם

נָתְנוּ יְדֵיהֶם אֶל זְמַנֶּךְ

וַיֹּאמְרוּ אֵלָיו מְשָׁל־בָּנוּ

כִּי בַגְּבִיר תָּרוּם יְמִינֶךְ

כָּבוֹד יְעַטוּהוּ וְיֹאמְרוּ לוֹ

קוּם הַזְּמַן וּלְבַשׁ עֶדְיֶךְ.

קוּם הַזְּמַן וּלְבַשׁ עֶדְיֶךְ

וּקְשׁוֹר שְׁבִיסֵי שַׁהֲרֹנֶיךְ

עַד אָן תְּנַצֵּל עֶדְיְךָ עַד אָן

תִּפְשֹׁט לְפָנֵינוּ סְדִינֶיךְ

אִם אֵין לְךָ נֵזֶר לְהִתְנוֹסֵס

כִּי חֻלְּלוּ נִזְרֵי צְפוּנֶיךְ

מֵעִם שְׁמוּאֵל קַח רְבִידֵי פָז

יִהְיוּ לְךָ עַל צַוְּרֹנֶיךְ

יָצִיץ בְּךָ שִׁירוֹ כְּמוֹ אֵטוּן

גִּיל וַעֲלֹז וּמְשֹׁךְ אַטוּנֶיךְ

דָּרַךְ בְּךָ כוֹכָב צָלַח וּרְכַב

כִּי בָא אֲשֶׁר יָאִיר אֱשׁוּנֶיךְ

EVERY AGE since time's beginning

gives its hand to this, your age,

and says to it, "Rule over us,

for by this prince, you have dominion!"

Decking it in glory, they proclaim:

"Arise, O age, put on your ornaments!"

ODE

ARISE, O AGE, put on your ornaments,

tie on your crescent anklets.

How long will you go unadorned,

how long robeless in our presence?

If you've no crown to flaunt, if men

have cast away your treasured diadems,

go to Samuel to get the golden necklaces

to place upon your throat.

Let his poems be your gleaming garment.

Draw that linen to yourself in joy.

A star has crossed your sky. Mount and ride!

The man to brighten up your darkness has arrived.

163

גָּבַהּ בְּרוֹשׁ תִּדְהָר בְּבֵית יִצְהָר
עַל נַעֲצוּצֵי קִמְשֹׁנֶיךָ
צָמַח לְךָ חֹרֶשׁ מְאֹד מֵצַל
פְּנֵה לְפָנָיו קִיקְיוֹנֶיךָ
נִקְרָא לְךָ הַיּוֹם יְאוֹר אֵיתָן
רַוֵּה בְמֵימָיו צִמְאוֹנֶךָ

עוּרָה לְבָבִי מַה־לְּךָ נִרְדָּם
עוּרָה וְהָקֵץ רַעְיוֹנֶיךָ
כַּמָּה גְעַרְתִּיךָ לְבַל תּוֹסִיף
דַּעַת לְבַל יִרְבּוּ יְגוֹנֶיךָ
הָסֵר תְּלוּנָתֶךָ וְאַל תִּזְכֹּר
הַיּוֹם לְפָנַי עִצְבוֹנֶיךָ
הִכּוֹן לְךָ כִּי יֶשׁ־לְךָ הַיּוֹם
רִיב עִם בְּנֵי לֵוִי צְפוּנֶיךָ
הַקְרֵב לְעֻמָּתָם שְׂעִיר חַטָּאת
אוּלַי יְכֻפַּר בּוֹ עֲוֹנֶךָ

אָנָּא כְרוֹב מִמְשַׁח לָאַט עֲלֵי
עַד אֶעֱרֹךְ מִשְׁפָּט לְפָנֶיךָ
מַה־סּוֹד מְשׁוּגָתִי וּמַה־פְּשָׁעִי
כִּי תַעֲבִיר עֲלֵי חֲרוֹנֶיךָ

Teak and cypress grow among the Levites,
  rising high above your brambly thorns.
A shady grove is flourishing for you,
  so clear away those scrubby castor shrubs.
A river lies before you, ever flowing;
  let its waters satisfy your thirst.

Wake up, my heart! What do you mean by sleeping?
  Arise and activate your mind.
How often have I warned you to eschew
  excessive learning and its misery!
Leave off complaining! Do not spend today
  telling me your tribulations.
Get ready, for today's the confrontation
  with your intimates, the sons of Levi.
Offer them a goat of expiation,
  something that may gain you pardon for your sin.

Majestic angel! Let me have a moment
  to lay my case before you.
What really is my error, my misdeed
  that you should swamp me with your anger?

תִּכְתָּב־לְךָ סֵפֶר כְּאִישׁ מָדוֹן
גַּם תַּאֲרִיךְ עָלַי לְשׁוֹנֶךָ
תַּרְעֵם בְּקוֹל גָּדוֹל אֲשֶׁר לֹא כֵן
לִהְיוֹת שְׁאוֹן רַעַשׁ סְאוֹנֶךָ
אַל תַּחֲשֹׁב כִּי צָלְלוּ אָזְנַי
יוֹם הַעֲלוֹת בָּם שַׁאֲנָנֶךָ
לוּ רָצְתָה נַפְשִׁי לְהִתְבָּאֵשׁ
אָז שָׂחֲקוּ מֵימֵי אֲבָנֶיךָ
הִנֵּה בְּחַר מִשְׁפָּט וְדַע מַה־טּוֹב
דּוּן כִּי אֲנִי חָפֵץ בְּדִינֶךָ

עַל מַה־תְּרִיבֵנִי פְּלִיל צֶדֶק
כִּי תַאֲרִיךְ בִּי קַלְשׁוֹנֶךָ
כִּמְעַט חֲשַׁבְתִּיךָ לְמִגְדַּל עֹז
עַד נָפְלוּ עָלַי אֲבָנֶיךָ
כִּמְעַט קְרָאתִיךָ זְמֹרַת זָר
עֵת נֶהְפְּכוּ לִי נַעֲמָנֶיךָ
תִּצְמָא לְךָ נַפְשִׁי וַתַּשְׁקֵנִי
תַּחַת צְמָאִי רֹאשׁ פְּתָנֶיךָ
אֶזְרַע לְפִי חֶסֶד וְתָשִׂים אֶת־
רֵאשִׁית תְּבוּאָתִי בְּגָרְנֶךָ
מַה־זֶּה גְּבִיר מַה־זֶּה וְעַל מַה־זֶּה
תִּצְפֹּן כְּמוֹ אֵלֶּה לְבָנֶיךָ

Why do you indite complaints, litigiously,

　　stretch out a hostile tongue at me,

thunder at me? Surely it's not right

　　that such a man as you should thunder!

Do not think my ears begin to ring

　　the moment that your clamor reaches them.

Besides, if I were willing to annoy you,

　　my stream of words would wear away your stones.

All right. Take me to court, decide what's best.

　　Judge me. I look forward to your judgment.

Why do you arraign me, righteous judge?

　　Why do you thrust your pitchfork at me?

I almost took you for a mighty tower,

　　but then your stones fell down on me.

I almost took you for a most exotic vine,

　　but then your lovely plants turned bad on me.

It's you my soul is thirsting for, but all

　　you let me drink to quench my thirst is venom.

I sow generosity, but you

　　seize my best crops for your own threshing-floor.

What has happened, lord? Why harbor

　　thoughts like these against your children?

תָּרוּץ בְּלִי עָוֹן וְתִכּוֹנֵן

לִקְרַאת שְׁלָמֶיךָ אֱמוּנֶיךָ

תִּגְאֶה וְכַשַּׁחַל תְּצוּדֵנִי

עַד כִּי תְכַלֶּה־בִּי שְׁנוּנֶיךָ

אִם הָאֱלֹהִים הוּא הֱסִיתְךָ בִּי

יָרַח קְטֹרֶת עַד רְצוֹנֶךָ

אוֹ אִם בְּנֵי אָדָם אֲרוּרִים הֵם

כִּי גֵרְשׁוּנִי מִלְּפָנֶיךָ

יַכְרֵת אֱלֹהִים דִּבְרֵי כָזָב

הַקֹּרְצִים בֵּינִי וּבֵינֶךָ

כִּי פָרְשׂוּ רֶשֶׁת לְיַד מַעְגָּל

וַיְבַעֲרוּ עָלַי עֲשָׁנֶיךָ

זָדוּ כְּמוֹ צִיבָא בְּבֶן־שָׁאוּל

וַיְדַבְּרוּ שֶׁקֶר בְּאָזְנֶיךָ

מִי זֶה אֲשֶׁר יָרִים בְּךָ יָדוֹ

אֵי זֶה זְבוּב יַבְאִישׁ שְׁמָנֶיךָ

מֵרִים בְּךָ יָדוֹ כְּמֵרִים יָד

בִּשְׁנֵי בְנֵי עַמְרָם קְצִינֶיךָ

הַשִּׁיר הֲלֹא לָכֶם בְּנֵי לֵוִי

וּלְךָ לְבַד מִתַּחְכְּמֹנֶיךָ

נָפַל לְךָ חֶבֶל בְּסוֹד הֵימָן

וּבְסוֹד בְּנֵי אָסָף מְבִינֶיךָ

You persecute where there's no sin,

    and take up arms against your allies,

intimidate me, stalk me like a lion,

    exhaust your stock of pointed arrows on me.

If it's God Who has incited you against me,

    I hope He will accept my incense,

    restore me to your favor,

but if this is the work of men, I curse them

    for driving me away from you.

May God strike down mendacious men who carry

    slanders back and forth between us,

who spread a net beside my path,

    who make you burn and smoke against me.

They've done to me what Ziba did to Mephibosheth—

    spoke slander in your ears.

Who would raise a hand against you? Where's the fly

    that could befoul your unguents?

To raise a hand against you is to raise a hand

    against the sons of Amram, those great chieftains.

O Levites, poetry is yours

    and, Samuel, yours especially among their sages.

Your lot is with the sons of Heman

    and Asaph, your masters.

אִם עָמְדוּ שָׂרִים בְּמִשְׁמַרְתָּם
הָיוּ נְגִידֵיהֶם סְגָנֶיךָ
יְשֻׁכַּל אֲבִי נָבָל אֲשֶׁר יַחְשֹׁב
לַעֲקֹר כְּצִיץ נֹבֵל אֲרָנֶיךָ
אֶשְׁלַף־לְךָ חַרְבִּי וְאֶגְעַר בּוֹ
סוּר פֶּן תְּגַלֶּה יַד קְלוֹנֶךָ
תֻּפַּח בְּאֵשׁ פֶּחָם וְגַם תִּזְרַק
בִּמְקוֹם חֲרֵרִים זַרְעֹנֶיךָ
תִּיגַע וְלֹא תוּכַל עֲלוֹת אֵלָיו
עַד תֶּאֱסֹף רוּחַ בְּחָפְנֶיךָ
הִנֵּה לְךָ עָלָיו שְׁנֵי עֵדִים
גַּם עוֹד שְׁלֹשָׁה נֶאֱמָנֶיךָ
הַתֹּם וְהַיּשֶׁר וְהַבִּינָה
זֶה מִלְּבַד שֵׁבֶט אֱמוּנֶיךָ

קוּם וַעֲטֵה הַשָּׂר מְעִיל כָּבוֹד
הִנֵּה אֲמָרַי פַּעֲמֹנֶיךָ
הַעַל תְּהִלָּתִי אֲשֶׁר שָׁמָּה
רָבִיד מְקֻשָּׁר עַל גְּרוֹנֶךָ
אַחַת נְשָׂאתִיהָ כְּמוֹ תֹרֶן
לָשֵׂאת בְּרֹאשׁ כָּל־הַר תְּרָנֶיךָ
קוּם וַעֲדֵה גָאוֹן וְהִנָּשֵׂא
כִּי עַמְּךָ הִנֵּה בְמֹאזְנֶיךָ

If the Levites manned their posts today,
    their leaders would be your assistants.
May that scoundrel's father be bereaved,
    who'd want to see your oak uprooted.
I draw my sword at him on your behalf, and chide:
    "Get out, before you show the world your shame!
You might as well blow charcoals into flame,
    or sow your seed on sunbaked soil.
You cannot reach this man, for all you strive,
    until you grasp the wind in two cupped palms.
Two witnesses can testify on his behalf—
    three, in fact, on whom you can rely:
Integrity and Fairness and Intelligence;
    and what is more, a clan of faithful men."

Arise, my lord, and robe yourself in honor:
    my rhetoric will serve you as a bell.
Give honor to my panegyric, for it binds
    a chain of office round your throat.
And it's unique: I've raised it as a standard
    to set on all the hills that bear your flag.
Arise! Dress in pride and sit in state,
    for with you in the balance are your kin—

חֶבְרוֹן וְעֻזִּיאֵל וּמִישָׁאֵל
וּשְׁאָר בְּנֵי לֵוִי זְקֵנֶיךָ
הַנֹּשְׂאִים אָרוֹן עֲלֵי כָתֵף
הַשֹּׁמְרִים מִקְדַּשׁ אֲדֹנֶיךָ
תָּרוּם בְּךָ קֶרֶן סְפָרַד עוֹד
מִיּוֹם הֱיוֹתְךָ עַד זְקֵנֶיךָ
תַּרְחִיב בְּךָ פֶּה עַל בְּנֵי שִׁנְעָר
הַשֹּׁאֲבִים מִמַּעְיָנֶיךָ
מַה־תִּגְבְּהִי בָּבֶל וּמַה־תִּגְאִי
שִׁנְעָר בְּמָעוּזֵּי גְאוֹנֶיךָ
דַּע כִּי בְאַרְצֵנוּ חֲבַצֶּלֶת
לֹא נִמְצְאָה בִּנְאוֹת שָׁרוֹנֶךָ
שָׂרֵי פְלִילִיָּה לְךָ עַד כִּי
פֶּה פָּעֲרוּ נֶגֶד עֲדָנֶיךָ

אַל תַּחְשְׁבֵנִי כִּי בְרֹב תִּקְוָה
אַפִּיל תְּחִנָּתִי לְפָנֶיךָ
לֹא מֵאֲשֶׁר יִירָאֲךָ לִבִּי
לוּ כָכְבֵי שַׁחַק הֲמוֹנֶיךָ
הָאֵל יְהִי עִמָּךְ וְאַל יַעֲמֹד
שָׂטָן לְעוֹלָם עַל יְמִינֶךָ
וּמְצָא בְעֵינָיו חֵן וְשֵׂכֶל טוֹב
וּרְאֵה בְנֵי בָנִים לְבָנֶיךָ.

Hebron, Uziel, and Mishael,

    all your forebears, Levites to a man,

who bore the Tabernacle on their shoulders,

    kept the watches of the Holy Temple.

Thanks to you, Spain's horn has stayed aloft

    throughout your life, from youth until old age.

Because of you, she outdoes Babylon;

    their people draw their water at your well.

Why should you boast, Iraq? And why, Shinar, so proud

    of those two mighty geonim of yours?

I tell you, in our land there is a rose

    the likes of which your Sharon never saw.

The Torah sages are your witnesses:

    they face your Eden rivers openmouthed.

Do not assume I lay my prayer before you

    in undue confidence,

or that I'd fear you, even if the stars

    served at your command.

May God be with you always. May no slanderer

    come forward ever to accuse you.

May you find all favor and success

    and live to see your children's children thrive.

אֱמֹר לְפָנַי צְפִירַת הַתְּעוּדָה
וְהַצֶּפֶת אֲשֶׁר עַל רֹאשׁ יְהוּדָה
וְהַכִּידוֹן אֲשֶׁר שַׂמְתִּיו לְאָדוֹן
וְלֹא אֶשְׁאַל גְּאַל מִן הָעֲבֹדָה
אֲנִי נָקָח בְּיַד מִקָּח וּמִמְכָּר
כְּמוֹ צִפּוֹר אֲשֶׁר בַּפַּח לְכוּדָה
וְלֹא אוּכַל מְצֹא פִדְיוֹם כְּהַיּוֹם
לְבַקֵּר הַיְשִׁיבָה הַחֲמוּדָה
וְשָׁלַחְתִּי שְׁלוֹמִי עַל מְקוֹמִי
לְבַל תִּהְיֶה לְחַטָּאתִי פְּקֻדָּה
כְּאִישׁ לוֹ מֶצְאָה יָדוֹ שְׁתֵּי צֹאן
וְלָקַח לוֹ שְׁתֵּי תוֹרִים לְתוֹדָה.

SAY TO HIM—the Torah's crown,

the turban on Judaea's head,

my lance, my lord,

the man I serve and never wish to leave:

I'm all tied up in business,

tangled as a netted bird.

I cannot find a way to get away

in order to attend your gathering.

I'm sending you this greeting in my place,

in order that you not find fault with me,

like one who can't afford a pair of sheep,

and makes a pair of doves his offering.

תְּרִיבוּן אִישׁ אֲשֶׁר לוּלֵי דְמָעָיו
קְרָבָיו נִשְׂרְפוּ מֵאֵשׁ צְלָעָיו
אֲמַרְתֶּם דֹּם וְהִתְאַפֵּק וְדַי כִּי
בְּאֹרֶךְ הַנְּדֹד כָּלוּ דְמָעָיו
וְדַל מֵרֹב־חֳלִי עַד כִּי נְשָׂאוֹ
זְבוּב קָטָן בְּאַחַד מִזְּרֹעָיו
וְהֹמֶה בַבְּכִי תָמִיד כְּאִלּוּ
פְרָת עֵינָיו וְכִנֹּרוֹת בְּמֵעָיו
וְצִידָיו הֶפְכוּ עָלָיו לְבָבוֹ
וְנֶהְפְּכוּ עֲלֵי אַרְצוֹ רְקִיעָיו
וְנָדַר אַחֲרֵי בֶגֶד יְדִידוֹ
וְלֹא עָלָה עֲלֵי עֶרֶשׂ יְצוּעָיו

הֲבָגַדְתָּ יְדִידִי בָּאֲהָבִים
וְאֵיכָה אִישׁ אֱמֶת יִבְגֹּד בְּרֵעָיו

YOU QUARREL with a man whose tears

    are all that keep the fire in his heart

    from burning up his entrails.

"Control yourself, be quiet!"—is what you say,

    as if it weren't bad enough

    that separation has exhausted all his tears,

that illness has emaciated him

    so badly that a fly could pick him up

    with just one arm.

He murmurs as he weeps

    as if his eyes contained the whole Euphrates,

    as if he had a bellyful of lutes.

His pains have overturned him,

    turned his earth to sky, his sky to earth.

Since his friend betrayed him, he has sworn

    never again to seek repose in sleep.

Have you betrayed our love, my friend?

    How can a man of truth betray his friends?

וּמִיּוֹם סוּרְךָ לֹא סָר יְגוֹנִי

וְהִצִּיב הַכְּאֵב עָלַי כְּרָעָיו

שְׁאַל יַעֵל לְעַפְעַפַּי וְיַגִּיד

אֲשֶׁר הִמְסוּ בְמֵימֵיהֶם סְלָעָיו

אֲהַבְתַּנִי וְהָיָה לִבְּךָ לִי

כְּלֵב זָקֵן לְיֶלֶד שַׁעֲשׁוּעָיו

נְטַעְתַּנִי וְאַחַר כֵּן תְּמָאֵן

וְאֵיךְ יַעֲקֹר אֱנוֹשׁ חָכָם נְטָעָיו

וְאֵיךְ תִּגְרַע וְתִמְנַע הַיְדִידֹת

וְאַתָּה מִנְּדִיבֵי עַם וְשׁוֹעָיו

וְאֵיכָה מִמְּךָ חִשְׁקוֹ יְכַסֶּה

לְבָבִי וַאֲנִי אֵדַע פְּשָׁעָיו

וְלוּ כָתַב לְךָ סֵפֶר יְרִיבוֹת

קְרַעְתִּיהוּ וְשָׂרַפְתִּי קְרָעָיו

בְּאַנְשֵׁי רִיב יְהִי חֶרֶץ וְכָלָה

וְיָשׁוּף הַזְּמַן רָאשֵׁי צְפָעָיו

אֲשֶׁר פָּתְחוּ כְּמוֹ חֶרֶב לְשׁוֹנָם

וְכַקַּשׁ נֶחְשְׁבוּ אַבְנֵי קְלָעָיו

וְאַל יַשִּׂיאֲךָ מֵהֶם שְׁלוֹמָם

הֲיַשִּׂיא מֵחֲמַת תַּנִּין צְבָעָיו.

Since you left, distress has never left me;

    pain has planted both its feet on me.

Ask the mountain goat about my eyes: he will tell you

    how their torrent turned his cliff to mud.

And yet you loved me. You were attached to me

    the way an old man loves his late-born child.

You planted me, then spurned me;

    what man of sense tears up his plantings?

How can you be niggardly with friendship—

    you, the source of all our people's bounty?

How can my heart conceal its love from you—

    I, who know its sins?

If it arraigned you with a bill of charges,

    I'd tear that bill to bits and burn its scraps.

May the querulous be ruined and destroyed.

    May Time trample on their vipers' heads.

They unsheathed their tongues like swords,

    and yet their hurling-stones are merely straw to me.

When they greet you, don't be taken in:

    Would you let a serpent's colored stripes

    distract you from its venom?

עֲזֹב הֶגְיוֹן בְּמַהֲלַל כָּל־סְגָנִים
וְאַל תִּתְהַר בְּנִרְגָּנִים וְשׁוֹנִים
וְהוֹדֵה רַב יְקוּתִיאֵל לְבַדּוֹ
בְּנוֹ יִצְחָק אֲדֹנֵי הָאֲדֹנִים
אֲשֶׁר לָבַשׁ תְּהִלָּה כַּמְּעִילִים
וְעָטָה הוֹד כְּמַעֲטֵה הַסְּדִינִים

עֲנִיתִיהוּ וְרַעְיוֹנַי נְבֻכִים
וְאֵין בִּי לַעֲנוֹת כֹּחַ וְאוֹנִים
לְאַט עָלַי וְתֵן פּוּגָה לְלִבִּי
הֲיָם אָנִי וְאִם כֹּחִי אֲבָנִים
בְּיַעַן כִּי הֲלָמוּנִי כְאֵבִים
הֲדָפוּנִי אֲפָפוּנִי יְגוֹנִים
וְהִנֵּה הֶחֱלִי בִּלָּה בְשָׂרִי
וְהִכְאִיב לֵב וְהִבְהִיל רַעְיוֹנִים
וְאֶתְגַּלְגַּל בְּצִירִים עַל יְצוּעַי
כְּמִתְגַּלְגֵּל עֲלֵי קוֹצִים וְצִנִּים
וְיָגַעְתִּי בְּאַנְחָתִי וְאֵידִי
וְנִלְאֵיתִי נְשֹׂא תּוּגוֹת וְאוֹנִים

"QUIT SINGING hymns to other courtiers.
    Don't be involved with miscreants and scoundrels.
Praise no one but Yekutiel,
    the son of Isaac, prince of princes,
who wears his praises like a robe of office,
    dons splendor like a chieftain's gown."

I answered—but my thoughts were muddled—
    I hardly had the strength to speak:
Go gently with me, let me catch my breath!
    Am I an ocean? Am I hard as rock?
Pains have hammered me,
    grief has beset me, smothered me,
and now my flesh is wasted by disease
    that keeps my heart in pain, my mind confused.
I toss in agony among my bedclothes
    like someone rolling on a bed of thorns.
I wear myself out groaning in my agony.
    I cannot bear such misery and sorrow.

וְקָם עָלַי כְּאַכְזְרֵי זְמַנִּי
וְיָרֶד־בִּי לְמַעֲמַקֵּי שְׁאוֹנִים
וְכָשַׁלְתִּי וְנָפַלְתִּי בְרִשְׁתּוֹ
וּמִכְמַרְתּוֹ וּפַחָיו הַטְּמֻנִים
זְמַן בֶּגֶד אֲשֶׁר בִּגְדִים יֶאֱהַב
וְשָׁב אֶל כָּל־בְּלִיַּעַל בְּפָנִים
וְכָפַת כָּל־נְדִיבֵי עָם יְיַבֵּשׁ
וּבָדֵי הַנְּבָלִים רַעֲנַנִּים
הֲכִי כִּי לַפְּתָאיִם הַנְּבָלִים
תְּהִלַּת חֵן וְהוֹד לֹא לַנְּבוֹנִים
לְזֹאת אַךְ יֶחֱרַד לִבִּי וְיִתַּר
אֲמָרַר בַּבְּכִי כִּבְנוֹת יְעֵנִים
וְעָלָיו אֶעֱשֶׂה מִסְפֵּד כְּתַנִּים
וְעָלָיו נוֹזְלֵי עֵינַי כְּעֵנִים
וְעַל בְּגָדִים אֲשֶׁר בָּגְדוּ כְנַחַל
וְעָפוּ אֶל אֲרֻבָּתָם כְּיוֹנִים
וְהַמַּעְיָן אֲשֶׁר קֶדֶם אֲדָמֶה
לְרַוּוֹתוֹ כְּמֵימֵי צִמְאוֹנִים
בְּחַנְתִּיהוּ וְהִנֵּה הוּא כְאַכְזָב
וּמֵימָיו נֶהְפְּכוּ לִי רֹאשׁ פְּתָנִים
וְהַכֶּרֶם אֲשֶׁר שֹׂרֵק חֲשַׁבְתִּיו
וְדִמִּיתִי נְטָעָיו נַעֲמָנִים

Time confronts me like a monster,

      drags me down to depths of horror.

I tripped and fell into his net,

      into his trap, into his hidden snares.

Time, the traitor, Time the traitor-lover

      turns a cheerful face to every villain,

dries up the boughs of nobles

      but leaves the twigs of villains ever verdant.

Adoring praise and glamour goes

      to mindless blackguards, never to the wise.

This throws my heart into a panic, sets it twitching,

      makes me wail like the ostriches.

 I howl like jackals, and my eyes

      gush tears in streams like fountains,

for traitors fail you like a wadi's water;

      they flit away like doves to cotes.

The fount that once I fancied

      would let me drink away my thirst,

turned fickle when I tested it—

      its water turned to adders' venom.

The vineyard with the vines that once seemed choice,

      the plantings that I thought delightful

בְּחָקְרִי אֶת־יְנִיקוֹתָיו מְצָאתִים

זְמֹרַת זָר וְסוּרֵי הַגְּפָנִים

אֲקַוֶּה לַעֲשׂוֹת עֵנָב וְעָשָׂה

בְּאָשִׁים וַחֲרֻלִּים קִמְּשֹׂנִים

מְכָרַנִי וְהֵפֵר אֶת־בְּרִיתִי

אֲהַבְתִּיהוּ וְלֹא שָׁמַר אֱמוּנִים

וְהַנֶּחְשָׁב בְּתוֹךְ אַנְשֵׁי שְׁלוֹמִי

אֲשֶׁר בָּטַח לְבָבִי בוֹ לְפָנִים

וְהָיִיתִי כְּמוֹ שֵׂכִים בְּעֵינָיו

וְאֶל צִדָּיו וּבִלְבָבוֹ צְנִנִים.

turned out, upon inspection, to be full
> of spurious and unproductive vines.
I hoped for grapes, but nothing did they yield
> but shriveled fruit and prickly thorns.
He sold me, broke my pact with him.
> I loved him, but he did not keep my faith.
The man preeminent among my friends,
> the one I always trusted in the past—
I'm nothing but a thorn stuck in his eye,
> stuck in his side, a bramble in his heart.

אֱמֹר לַשַּׂר אֲשֶׁר עָלָה וְגָבַר
וְנִכְבָּדוֹת בְּתֵבֵל בּוֹ מְדֻבָּר
בְּךָ בָּטַח וְלֹא נֶעְזַר לְבָבִי
אֲבָל בּוֹשׁ מֵאֲשֶׁר קִנָּה וְשִׂבָּר
כְּבַת נָדִיב בְּעֵת פָּתְחָה לְדוֹדָהּ
וְהוּא חָמַק לְפָנֶיהָ וְעָבָר.

TELL A COURTIER who rose to power,

    whose fame is talked of universally:

My heart relied on you, but got no help.

    It found not what it hoped for, but frustration,

like a princess when she opened for her love,

    and found that he had slipped away and gone.

הֲלֹא צִוָּה אֲבִי כָל־הַחֲכָמִים
בְּסִפְרוֹ אַל תְּהִי אִישׁ רִיב וּמָדוֹן
וְאַתָּה רִיב וּמִדְיָנִים תְּחַרְחַר
וְתַרְבֶּה חֵטְא וְגַם פֶּשַׁע וְזָדוֹן
יְרָא מֵחֵץ מְאֹד שָׁחוּט וְשָׁנוּן
וְגוּרָה מִלַּהַב חֶרֶב וְכִידוֹן
אֱהִי עַבְדְּךָ שְׁלוֹמִים אִם תְּבַקֵּשׁ
וְאִם לָרִיב אֱהִי לְךָ שַׂר וְאָדוֹן.

THE FATHER of all sages ordered us
>to keep away from strife and bickering.
Yet you go picking fights and altercations,
>besides committing every heinous sin.
Beware an arrow sharp and highly honed;
>beware the blazing blade of sword and spear.
If peace you want, I'll gladly be your slave,
>but if we fight, I'll end up as your master.

הֲתִלְעַג לֶאֱנוֹשׁ יָחִיד בְּדוֹרוֹת

וְתִבְזֶה אִישׁ אֲשֶׁר לָבַשׁ יְקָרוֹת

אֲשֶׁר הַתֹּם וְהַיּשֶׁר לְבוּשׁוֹ

וּבָחַר בֶּאֱמוּנָה מִבְּחֻדוֹרוֹת

אֲשֶׁר לִבּוֹ כְּחוֹל יִכָּבֵד בְּיוֹם בֻּז

וְיוֹם עֶבְרָה וְיוֹם שָׁאוֹן וְצָרוֹת

אֲרָזִים לֹא עֲמָמֻהוּ וְכַפָּיו

כְּכָל־אַנְשֵׁי יְקָר נָשֵׁם נְעוּרוֹת

בְּלִבּוֹ נִפְלָאוֹת חָכְמָה וּמוּסָר

וְהַדֵּעוֹת בְּנַפְשׁוֹ הֵם סְתוּרוֹת

לֵךְ אֱמֹר לְאִישׁ שְׂפָתֵי מְחִתָּה

אֲשֶׁר הֶבֶל וְרוּחַ בָּם צְרוּרוֹת

שְׁמַע מֶנִּי וְהַטֵּה אָזְנְךָ לִי

וְקוּם וּבְרַח וְעָבְרָה מֵעֲבָרוֹת

בְּטֶרֶם לֹא אֲשִׂימְךָ נָע כְּשִׁכּוֹר

בְּצִיר יַכְאִיב לְבָבְךָ כַּמְצֵרוֹת

וְתָחִיל בַּחֲמַת חִצֵּי אֲמָרַי

כְּמַבְכִּירָה עֲצוּרָה בַּנְּעָרוֹת

AND DO YOU mock a man unique in any age?
>And do you scorn a person robed in dignity,
attired in probity and innocence,
>committed since he was a boy to loyalty?
A man whose heart is heavy as the sand when he is scorned,
>when facing anger, trouble, and disaster?
A man whom even cedars do not overshadow,
>whose palms are clean, like men of worth and reputation?
A man whose heart is full of wondrous wisdom
>and in whose soul are buried doctrines true?

To you—a man of timid lips that harbor
>nonsense and vapidity—I say:
Incline your ear to me, take my advice.
>Get up and get away, evade the rage,
before I set you stumbling like a drunk,
>put your heart in pain severe as birth pangs;
before my darts, word-poisoned, make you thrash about
>as if you were a woman in midlife,
>enduring her first labor.

וְאִם הִנֵּה וְלִי יָמִים מְעַטִּים
וְשֵׁשׁ עֶשְׂרֵה שְׁנוֹתַי בָּם סְפוּרוֹת
דְּעֶה כִּי גָדְלוּ דַרְכֵי נְתִיבַי
וּבַל אֹחֵז אֲבָל כִּי בַמְּקֹרוֹת
וְהִנֵּה כֵן יְבָרֶךְ כָּל־חֲכַם לֵב
וְכָל־נֶפֶשׁ תְּבַקֵּשׁ הַבְּצָרוֹת
וְלִי שִׁיר שֶׁיִּפְצֵץ צוּר בְּעֻזּוֹ
וְיוֹצִיא מִסְּלָעִים הַנְּהָרוֹת
וְדַלְתֵי הַתְּבוּנָה נִפְתְּחוּ לִי
וְהֵם אֶל כָּל־בְּנֵי עַמִּי סְגוּרוֹת
וְלִי דֶרֶךְ מְסֻקָּל בַּשְּׁחָקִים
וְגַם לִי מַחֲנֶה עִם הַמְּאוֹרוֹת

אֲבָל עוּרָה לְךָ יָשֵׁן וְנִרְדָּם
וְנֶפֶשׁ מִנַּפְשׁוֹת הַשְּׁכוּרוֹת
בְּלִי דַעַת בְּלִי שֵׂכֶל אֲבָל כִּי
לְחֶרְפָּה תּוֹךְ גְּוִיָּתָם אֲסוּרוֹת
וְאִם עַל חִכְּךָ מַר הַדְּבַשׁ קוּם
אֱכֹל וּשְׁתֵה לְשָׂבְעָה מַמְּרוֹרוֹת
וְהָעִוֵּר יְמַשֵּׁשׁ בַּחֲשֵׁכָה
לְמַעַן מָאֲסוּ עֵינָיו בָּאוֹרוֹת
וְתֵלֶךְ כַּאֲבֵל־אֵם וַחֲפוּי רֹאשׁ
וְיוּסַר מֵעֲלֵי רֹאשְׁךָ עֲטָרוֹת

And though my years are not so very many—
     sixteen years is what I count, in all—
know this: my course is lofty.
     I reach for nothing lower than the roof-beams,
for thus are blessed the wise at heart
     and all who strive for the impossible.
I have poems strong enough to split
     flint, to bring forth rivers out of rock.
Wisdom's doors are open wide to me,
     doors not open to just anyone.
I have a well-paved path among the heavens,
     a camp among the luminaries.

So wake up, drowser, sleeper,
     soulmate of inebriates,
of mindless men devoid of intellect,
     with minds locked shamefully inside their bodies.
Is honey bitter to your taste? Go gobble,
     guzzle bitters to your heart's content.
Let the blind man feel his way in darkness,
     since his eyes despise the light.
Go about like one who mourns his mother,
     bareheaded and devoid of ornaments.

קְרָא שִׁירַי וְאַל תִּדְאַג לְמַעַן
חֲרָפוֹת בּוֹ בְךָ יִהְיוּ קְשׁוּרוֹת
לְמַעַן כִּי אֲנִי אָשׁוּב וְאֶשְׁכַּח
נְטֹר אֵיבָה וְאַקְשִׁיב הָעֲתָרוֹת
וְלִי מַרְפֵּא לְכָל־מַכָּה אֲנוּשָׁה
וּמִדְּבָרֵי צֱרִי עַל כָּל־מְזֹרוֹת
אֲבָל כִּי עַל מְנָת תָּשׁוּב וְכָל־יוֹם
תְּלַחֵךְ מִנַּעֲלֵי הָעֲפָרוֹת
וְכֵן אָשׁוּב אֲנִי אָז לָךְ וְיִהְיוּ
אֲמָרַי הַנְּעִימִים לָךְ כְּתָרוֹת
וְאָשִׂים מַעֲלוֹתֶיךָ גְּבֹהוֹת
עֲלֵי שָׂרִים וְיִהְיוּ בָם יְתֵרוֹת.
וְשָׂרֵי הָאֲלָפִים יִכְרְעוּ לָךְ
וְהַמֵּאוֹת וְשָׂרֵי הָעֲשָׂרוֹת
וְאִמְרוֹתַי אֲשֶׁר עַתָּה חֲקַקְתִּים
יְהוּ בִלְשׁוֹן מְתֵי מוּסָר זְכוּרוֹת
וּבִידֵיהֶם יְהוּ לָהֶם שְׁבָטִים
לְיַסֵּר הַפְּתָאִים בָּם לְדֹרוֹת

194

וְחִבַּרְתִּי בְךָ אֵלֶּה לְיַסֵּר
לְבַב נִמְהָר בְּאֵלֶּה הַהֲדוּרוֹת
וְעֵת תָּבֹא בְמִלְחָמָה תְּשַׁנֵּס
חֲלָצֶיךָ וְתַחְגֹּר עֹז חֲגֹרוֹת

Peruse my poem. Do not mind
    that it will tie your name to insults,
for I can yet relent, nor forever will I
    harbor hatred. I heed supplication.
I have a cure for every grievous wound;
    my speech is balm for every ailment—
but on condition that you come to me
    and lick the dust each morning from my shoes.
Then I will return to you in turn.
    My words will be a crown upon your head.
I will extol your virtues over those
    of other princes—yes, outdo their praises.
Generals will genuflect to you,
    not to mention lesser officers.
These words of mine that I have put in verse
    will be remembered by all cultured men,
to serve as truncheons in their hands
    forevermore for disciplining fools.

I've written you these verses to admonish
    a heart impetuous with lovely lines.
When you go forth to battle, gird your loins
    and bind yourself about in belts of valor.

וְעוֹד אָשִׁיר לְבַד אֵלֶּה בִּשְׁמֶךָ

וְאֶשְׁלַח אֶל קְצֵה תֵבֵל אֲחֵרוֹת

וְאִם בִּלְבָבְךָ שֶׁמֶץ תְּבוּנָה

הֲלֹא תֵדַע יְקָר שָׁרִים וְשָׁרוֹת

וְאִם אַתָּה חֲסַר שֵׂכֶל וּבִינָה

וְדֵעוֹת מִלְּבָבְךָ עֲדוּרוֹת

בְּעֵינֵי כָל־אֱנוֹשׁ יַשְׂכִּיל וְיָבִין

אֲנִי פָטוּר וְשִׁירוֹתַי פְּטוּרוֹת.

Then I will sing yet other songs of you
     and others still that I will send abroad.
If you have any wisdom in your heart,
     you'll know the worth of poets and of singers.
But if your wit and wisdom are deficient,
     if your mind's devoid of doctrines true,
then in the eyes of all clear-thinking men,
     my verse and I disclaim responsibility.

וְאַהֲבָתִי וְשִׁבְרִי שֶׁבְּלִבִּי

וְעֶצֶם אַהֲבָתִי לִי יְשַׁלֵּם

וְהִנֵּךְ הֲקַלּוֹתָ אֲהָבִי

וְאֵלַי לֹא הֲשִׁיבוֹתָ גְּמוּלָם

וְשֵׁרַתַּנִי בְּעֵין קָלוֹן כְּשׁוּרֵךְ

נִמְבְּזֶה וַחֲדַל אִישִׁים וְנִפְלָם

אֱמֶת כִּי עֵינְךָ טָח מֵרְאוֹתִי

וְאוֹרִי מִמְּךָ נִסְתָּר וְנֶעְלָם

וְאִישׁ עִוֵּר שְׁתָם עַיִן הֲיִרְאֶה

מְאוֹר שֶׁמֶשׁ וְיָרֵחַ בְּהֶלְם

הֲלֹא אוֹרִי פְּנֵי תֵבֵל יְכַסֶּה

וְיַגִּיעַ עֲדֵי שִׁנְעָר וְעֵילָם

וְלִי לֵבָב כָּחוֹל יִכְבַּד בְּיוֹם בּוּז

וְיֶהֱמֶה כַּהֲמוֹת יַמִּים וְגַלָּם

וְלוּ יֵקָלוֹן כְּבוֹדִי הַמְּאוֹרִים

אֲשֶׁר בִּמְעוֹן שְׁמֵי מָרוֹם זְבֻלָם

גְּעַלְתִּימוֹ וְלָעַד לֹא זְכַרְתִּים

וּפָנַי לֹא הֲסִבֹּתִי לְמוּלָם

אֲנִי אֶרֶץ לְמִדְעִי אֲמוּנִי

שְׁלָמִי וַעֲפַר רַגְלַי לְרַגְלָם

THE LOVE and hope abiding in my heart
    and all the love I bear should be returned.
But you have taken my affection lightly
    and not requited me as I deserve.
You glare at me with that contempt you'd show
    to any derelict or tramp.
Your eye might just as well be smeared with plaster,
    since my light's invisible to you.
Can a blind man with his two blank eyes
    see the sunlight or the moonlight glistening?
My light irradiates the whole world's face
    as far as Babylonia and Persia.
My heart is heavy as the sand when scorned.
    It surges like the sea with all its breakers.
Even if the sun and moon on high
    gave offense against my dignity,
I would revile them. I'd cut them dead,
    and never turn my face in their direction.
To loyal allies, to my friends,
    I'm solid earth, I'm dirt beneath their feet.

וּמִדְבָּרִי בְּלִבּוֹתָם כְּמַלְקוֹשׁ

וְכִשְׂעִירִים עֲלֵי דֶשֶׁא בְּנָזְלָם

אֲבָל שָׂחַק אֲנִי עַל רֹאשׁ מְשַׂנְאַי

וְאַמְטִיר אֵשׁ מְלַהֶטֶת יְבוּלָם

וְהֶחָפֵץ לְהַשִּׂיג מַעֲלָתִי

כְּחָפֵץ לַעֲלוֹת שַׁחַק בְּסֻלָּם

אֱמֶת מִנְעָל לְרַגְלֵי עָשׁ וְכִימָה

וְאָמְנָם כִּי שְׂרוֹךְ נַעֲלִי כְּסִילָם

וְעַתָּה הִנְנִי אַתִּיר אֲגֻדּוֹת

אֲהָבֶיךָ וְלֹא אַחֲזִיק בְּחֶבְלָם

וְאֶמְחֶה אֶת־שְׁמָךְ מֵעַל לְשׁוֹנִי

וְלֹא אָשׁוּב לְהַזְכִּירְךָ לְעוֹלָם.

My words fall on their hearts like rains of spring,
     like drops that trickle gently onto grass.
But to my foes, they're like a sky,
     raining, pouring flames upon their heads,
     consuming all their yield.
To try to reach my rank is tantamount
     to scaling heaven using just a ladder.
To me, the Bear and Pleiades are merely footwear,
     Orion just a lace to tie my boot.
I herewith sunder all our ties of friendship;
     no longer will I hold on to its bond.
I now eradicate you from my tongue.
     Never will I speak your name again.

שְׁמוּאֵל מֵת בְּנוֹ לַבְרָט

וְעָמַדְתָּ עֲלֵי כַנּוֹ

וְכָלִינוּ מְאֹד אֵלָיו

וְאוּלָם הִנְּךָ הִנּוֹ

וְלוּ יֵשׁ חַי תְּפַשְׂנוּהוּ

וְרָצַעְנוּ לְךָ אָזְנוֹ

הֲמִן הָעֵץ אֲשֶׁר מָנַע

אֱלֹהִים מֵעֲצֵי עֶדְנוֹ

תְּמַלֵּא בִטְנְךָ דַּעַת

וְתִתְעַדֵּן בְּטוּב דִּשְׁנוֹ

וְתִתְחַכַּם וְתֹאמַר כִּי

אֱלוֹהַּ עַז וְגַם קַנּוֹא

קְרָאָנוּ לְךָ שִׁיר שָׁם

בְּבֵין כִּימָה וְעָשׁ קַנּוֹ

וְלִשְׂמֹאלוֹ מְנַחֵם שָׁם

וְשָׁם אָבוּן לִימִינוֹ

וּמַה־נִּמְרָץ וּמַה־נַּעֱרָץ

בְּמִדְבָּרָיו וְעִנְיָנוֹ

וּמֵחֵשֶׁק שְׁלַחְנוּהוּ

בְּיַד כָּרִי לְאֶרֶץ נָא

O SAMUEL, old Dunash is no more,

    and you have come to take his place.

Yesterday, he was our man;

    today, you have become our he.

If he were living, we would seize him,

    bore his ear, make him your slave.

Did you fill yourself with wisdom,

    from the tree the Lord forbade

in His garden east of Eden

    so that, sated with its richness,

you would find the skill to write

    "O God of power! Raging God!"?

We've read your poem. It resides

    amid the Bear and Pleiades,

Menaḥem sitting at its left,

    Abun sitting at its right.

Vigorous it is, impressive

    in its wording and its matter.

We liked it so much that we sent it

    by a messenger to Egypt,

וְלַסֹּבֶא נְתַנּוּהוּ

לְהִתְרוֹנֵן בְּאַגָּנוּ

וּבֶן־גִּבּוֹר וּבֶן־חַיִל

כְּתַבְנוּהוּ בְמָגְנוּ

אֲהָהּ לַשִּׁיר אֲשֶׁר נָפַל

וְאֵין תִּקְוָה לְפִדְיוֹנוּ

בְּיַד אִישׁ יַעֲנֶה רוּחַ

וְקָדִים מָלְאָה בִטְנוֹ

וְכָל־עֶצֶם לְעַצְמוֹ שָׁב

וְכָל־מִין שָׁב אֱלֵי מִינוֹ.

gave it to our jolly tipplers
      to bellow it amid their cups,
had it graven on the shields
      of warriors and fighting men.

Woe betide a fallen poem,
      verses irredeemable,
by a man who chases wind,
      his belly full of vapor!
Truly, every substance seeks its own,
      and every like reverts to like!

אָמַרְתִּי לוּ שְׁקַלְתֶּם בַּכְּסָפִים
אֲזַי הָיוּ יְתֵרִים וַעֲדוּפִים
לְמַעַן הֵם כְּסַפִּירִים רְצוּפִים
וְכַטַּל מִשְּׁמֵי שַׁחַק עֲרוּפִים
וְרֹאשׁ בְּשֶׂם וּמֹר הֵמָּה נְטוּפִים
וְאַבְנֵי הַבְּדֹלַח בָּם סְחוּפִים
וְעֵת הֵמָּה דְּבַשׁ נֹפֶת וְצוּפִים
וְעֵת הֵם נְשָׁכִים כִּנְשֹׁךְ שְׂרָפִים
וּבָהֶם גֹּנְבֵי הַשִּׁיר יְעֵפִים
וְטֶרֶם יִגְּעוּ אֵלָיו שְׂרוּפִים
בְּחֹשֶׁךְ וַחֲלַקְלַקּוֹת הֲדוּפִים
וּמֵרָעָה אֱלֵי רָעָה דְּחוּפִים
וְאֵיךְ תַּשְׁווּ אֲרָיוֹת לַאֲלָפִים
יְשִׂימְכֶם אֵל בְּפִי אַרְיֵה טְרוּפִים.

IF YOU WOULD try to price my words,

    you'd see that they're beyond appraisal,

for they're like perfect rows of crystals,

    like the dew that drips from heaven.

Scented as if dripped with myrrh,

    sweeping gemstones in their flow.

Sometimes sweet as honeycomb,

    yet sometimes they can sting like vipers.

Poem-thieves can't handle them:

    their hands get scorched before they touch them.

Then they're pitched to slime and darkness,

    from disaster to disaster.

Lions you compare to cattle?

    So may you be ripped by lions!

הֲגָנַבְתָּ וְכִחַשְׁתָּ דְּבָרַי
וְחָתַרְתָּ וּפָרַצְתָּ גְּדֵרוֹת
וְקִוִּיתָ לְהִתְנַשֵּׂא בְּשִׁירַי
לְהִמָּצֵא לְךָ עֶזְרָה בְּצָרוֹת

הֲיוּכְלוּן לַעֲלוֹת שַׂחַק בְּנֵי אִישׁ
לְהַסְתִּיר מֵעֲלֵי תֵבֵל מְאוֹרוֹת
וְהַדָּבָר מְאֹד נָקֵל בְּעֵינַי
הֲיִבְשׁוּן מִדְּלִי אֶחָד יְאוֹרוֹת.

DID YOU DARE to plagiarize my verses,

    burrow under, break through boundary-fences,

use my lines for your aggrandizement,

    thinking they would help you out in trouble?

Can mere mortals rise into the sky

    and hide the sun and moon and stars from earthlings?

To me, your act of theft is nothing:

    Can a bucket empty out the ocean?

Nature, Wine,
and Eros

כָּתַב סְתָיו בִּדְיוֹ מְטָרָיו וּבִרְבִיבָיו
וּבְעֵט בְּרָקָיו הַמְּאִירִים וְכַף עָבָיו
מִכְתָּב עֲלֵי גַן מִתְכֵלֶת וְאַרְגָּמָן
לֹא נִתְכְּנוּ כָהֶם לְחֹשֵׁב בְּמַחְשָׁבָיו
לָכֵן בְּעֵת חָמְדָה אֲדָמָה פְּנֵי שַׁחַק
רָקְמָה עֲלֵי בַדֵּי עֲרוּגוֹת כְּכוֹכָבָיו.

WINTER WROTE with rains and showers for ink,

    with lightning for a pen and a hand of cloud,

a letter on the ground in blue and violet,

    a work no artisan could match with all his skill.

So when earth was longing for the sky,

    she wove upon her flower beds

    something like the stars.

יְשַׁלֵּם הַסְּתָו נִדְרוֹ וְיָקִים
דְּבָרוֹ לַחֲבַצֶּלֶת עֲמָקִים
וְיוֹם קַיִץ לְיַד חֹרֶף מְצֻפֶּה
יְבוֹאוּהוּ לְבַשֵּׂר הַבְּרָקִים
אֲשֶׁר תֵּלֵד בְּלִי עֶצֶב אֲדָמָה
וְהֶעָבִים יְלָדֶיהָ מְנִיקִים
רְאֵה כִּי שָׂחֲקָה תֵבֵל וְרַכּוּ
לְחָיֶיהָ אֲשֶׁר הָיוּ חֲזָקִים
וְכָסּוּ הָעֲרָגוֹת כָּתְנוֹת חוּר
וְשָׁנִי שִׁבְּצוּם עָבֵי שְׁחָקִים
וּמַרְאֵיהֶן כְּמַרְאֵה הַכְּתָמִים
וְגַבֵּיהֶן כְּגַבֵּי הַבְּרָקִים
וְקָם הַתּוֹר וְהֶעָגוּר וְהַסִּיס
לְהִתְפָּאֵר עֲלֵי יוֹנֵי אֲפִיקִים
וְעֵת כִּי יִתְּנוּ רֹאשָׁם לְקַפֵּץ
תְּדַמֶּה פַעֲמֵיהֶם בָּאֲזִקִּים
בְּהִגָּלוֹת הֲדַר שֶׁמֶשׁ עֲלֵיהֶם
יְכַסּוּ צַוְּרֹנֵיהֶם עֲנָקִים

WINTER KEPT its vow,

    fulfilled its promise to the lily of the valley.

A summer day had waited all through winter.

    Then the lightning came, proclaiming

that the earth had given painless birth

    and that her babes were nursing at the breasts of clouds.

Look how the earth is laughing, look how soft

    her cheeks, just yesterday so hard.

The beds are draped in coats woven of threads

    of white and red, interwoven by the clouds of heaven.

To the eye, they look like bits of gold;

    their backs resemble jaspers.

The pigeon, crane, and swallow rise and boast

    that they are better than the doves of the canals.

When they cock their heads and start to hop,

    you almost think their feet are caught in chains,

and when the splendid sunlight shines on them,

    they seem to put on colored neck-rings.

הִנֵּה בָּנוֹת עָגוּר אֲשֶׁר נוֹעֲדוּ

שָׁרוֹת עֲלֵי פֹארוֹת וְלֹא לָמְדוּ

אֵיךְ תִּשְׁמְעוּ קוֹלָם בְּגִנַּת אֱגוֹז

הֵלֵךְ וְלֹא תִשְׁתּוּ וְלֹא תֶחֱדוּ

מַה־טּוֹב עֲנָפִים חִדְּשָׁמוֹ זְמַן

חָדָשׁ וְנִצָּנִים בְּגַן יֻלְּדוּ

עֵת תַּעַבֹר עֲלֵיהֶם אֲזֵי

שִׂיחִים כְּשָׁחִים זֶה לְזֶה יִקְּדוּ.

LOOK! THE CRANES are gathered,

    singing on the boughs, though never taught.

Can you hear their song among the nut-trees

    and not rejoice and drink?

How lovely: boughs renewed in season new,

    and buds in gardens born,

Breezes blowing—bushes bowing,

    like gentlemen in earnest conversation.

לְכָה רֵעִי וְרֵעַ הַמְּאוֹרִים

לְכָה עַמִּי וְנָלִין בַּכְּפָרִים

וְהִנֵּה הַסְּתָו עָבַר וְנִשְׁמַע

בְּאַרְצֵנוּ הֲמוֹן סִיסִים וְתֹרִים

וְנִתְלוֹנֵן בְּצֵל רִמּוֹן וְתָמָר

וְתַפּוּחַ וְכָל־צִמְחֵי הֲדָרִים

וְנִתְהַלֵּךְ בְּצִלְלֵי הַגְּפָנִים

וְנִשְׁתּוֹקֵק רְאוֹת פָּנִים הֲדוּרִים

בְּאַרְמוֹן נַעֲלֶה מִכָּל־סְבִיבָיו

וְנִבְנָה בָּאֲבָנִים הַיְקָרִים

אֲשֶׁר תֻּכַּן עֲלֵי נָכוֹן שְׁתוֹתָיו

וְקִירוֹתָיו כְּמִגְדָּלִים בְּצוּרִים

וְיָצִיעַ מִישָׁר מִסְּבִיבָיו

שְׁרֹנִים פֵּאֲרוּ כָל־הַחֲצֵרִים

וְהַבָּתִּים בְּנוּיִם וַעֲדוּיִים

בְּפִתּוּחִים פְּתוּחִים וַאֲטוּרִים

מְרֻצָּפִים בְּאַבְנֵי שֵׁשׁ וָבַהַט

וְלֹא אוּכַל סְפֹר כַּמָּה שְׁעָרִים

COME WITH ME, let's spend a night in the country,

    my friend, you intimate of heaven's stars,

for winter's finally over—you can hear

    the doves and swallows chattering.

We'll lounge beneath the pomegranate trees,

    palm trees, apple trees,

    everything lovely and leafy,

stroll among the vines, and look with pleasure

    at all those splendid faces,

in a palace loftier than everything around it,

    built of noble stones,

solid, resting on thick foundations,

    with walls like towers fortified,

set upon a flat place, plains all around it

    splendid to look at from within its courts.

Chambers well-constructed, all adorned with carvings,

    open-work and closed-work,

paving of alabaster, paving of marble,

    gates so many, I cannot even count them!

וְדַלְתוֹתָם כְּדַלְתֵי הֵיכְלֵי שֵׁן

מָאֳדָמִים בְּאַלְגֻּמֵּי דְבִירִים

וְחַלּוֹנִים שְׁקוּפִים מֵעֲלֵיהֶם

שְׁמָשׁוֹת שָׁכְבוּ בָהֶם מְאוֹרִים

וְהַקֻּבָּה כְּאַפִּרְיוֹן שְׁלֹמֹה

תְּלוּיָה מַשְׂכִּיּוֹת הַחֲדָרִים

אֲשֶׁר תָּסֹב וְתִתְהַפֵּךְ בְּעֵינִי

בְּדָלְחִים וְסַפִּירִים וְדָרִים

וְזֶה בַּיּוֹם וּבָעֶרֶב דְּמוּתָהּ

כְּשַׂחֵק כּוֹכָבָיו בַּלֵּיל סְדוּרִים

וּבָהּ יִיטַב לְבַב כָּל־דָּשׁ וְעָמֵל

וְיִנְשׁוּ אוֹבְדִים רִישָׁם וּמָרִים

רְאִיתִיהָ וְשָׁכַחְתִּי עֲמָלִי

וְהִתְנַחֵם לְבָבִי מִמְּצָרִים

וְכִמְעַט קַט גְּוִיָּתִי תְעוֹפֵף

בְּשִׂמְחָתִי כְּעַל כַּנְפֵי נְשָׁרִים

וְיָם מָלֵא וְיִדְמֶה יָם שְׁלֹמֹה

אֲבָל לֹא יַעֲמֹד עַל הַבְּקָרִים

וּמַצַּב הָאֲרָיוֹת עַל שְׂפָתוֹ

כְּאִלּוּ שָׁאֲגוּ טֶרֶף כְּפִירִים

אֲשֶׁר קִרְבָּם כְּמַעְיָנִים יְפִיצוּן

עֲלֵי פִיהֶם זְרָמִים כַּנְּהָרִים

Doors like the portals of ivory palaces,
     red with cedar panels, like the Holy Temple.
Wide windows over them, and in those windows,
     the sun and moon and stars!
It has a dome, too, like Solomon's palanquin,
     suspended like a jewel-room,
turning, changing,
     pearl-colored, color of crystal and marble.
That's in daytime, but in the evening
     a veritable night sky, all set with stars.
It cheers the hearts of poor men, laborers;
     bitter men, failing men forget their want.
I saw it once and put aside my troubles.
     In it, my heart found comfort from distress,
my body seemed ready to fly away for happiness,
     as if on eagles' wings.

It had a basin brimming, like Solomon's basin,
     but not on the backs of bulls like his—
lions stood around its edge
     like whelps that roar for prey;
for they had wells inside them, wells that emitted
     water in streams through their mouths like rivers.

וְאַיָּלוֹת שְׁתוּלוֹת בַּתְּעָלוֹת

נְבוּבוֹת לִהְיוֹת מַיִם מְעָרִים

וְלֵרֹס הַצְּמָחִים בַּעֲרָגוֹת

וּבָאִים זֹרֵק מַיִם טְהֹרִים

וְגִנַּת הַהֲדַס בָּהֶם לְהַשְׁקוֹת

אֲמִירִים כַּעֲנָנִים הֵם וְזֹרִים

אֲשֶׁר רֵיחָם כְּרֵיחַ הַבְּשָׂמִים

כְּאִלּוּ הֵם מְקֻטָּרִים בְּמֹרִים

וְעוֹפוֹת יִתְּנוּ קוֹל בָּעֲפָאִים

וְנִשְׁקָפוֹת עֲלֵי כַפּוֹת תְּמָרִים

וְצִצִּים רַעֲנַנִּים נַעֲמָנִים

כְּשׁוֹשַׁנִּים נְרָדִים עִם כְּפָרִים

אֲשֶׁר מִתְפָּאֲרִים הֵם זֶה עֲלֵי זֶה

וְהֵם כֻּלָּם בְּעֵינֵינוּ בְּרוּרִים

וְאֹמְרִים הַכְּפָרִים כִּי אֲנַחְנוּ

לְבָנִים מְשִׁלִים עַל הַמְּאוֹרִים

וְהַיּוֹנִים מְנַהֲגוֹת בַּהֲגוֹתָן

וְאֹמְרוֹת נַחְנוּ שָׁרוֹת לְתֹרִים

אֲשֶׁר בָּהֶם נְכַשֵּׁף הַלְּבָבוֹת

לְמַעַן מִבְּדֹלָחִים יְקָרִים

וְקָמוּ הַצְּבָאִים כַּבְּתוּלוֹת

וְכִסּוּ אֶת־הֲדָרָן בַּהֲדָרִים

Then there were canals with does planted by them,

    does that were hollow, also pouring water,

sprinkling the plants in the garden beds,

    casting pure water over the clover,

while treetops, cloudlike,

    were sprinkling the myrtle garden.

It issued fragrance like a box of spices,

    as if someone had scented it with myrrh.

Birds sent their voices flying from the boughs,

    while peering through the palm-fronds,

and there were fresh blossoms of anemone,

    lily, saffron, camphor,

each one boasting that she was the best,

    (though we thought each was beautiful enough!).

The camphor blossoms said, "We are so white

    we dominate the sun and moon and stars!"

The doves complained at such talk and said,

    "No, we are the princesses here!

    Just see our neck-rings,

with which we charm the hearts of men,

    dearer far than pearls."

The bucks rose up against the girls

    and darkened their splendor with their own,

וְגַם הִתְפָּאֲרוּ יַחַד עֲלֵיהֶן
לְמַעַן הֵם כְּאַיָּלִים צְעִירִים
וְעֵת כִּי נַעֲלָה שֶׁמֶשׁ עֲלֵיהֶן
עֲנִיתִיו דֹּם וְאַל תַּעֲבֹר מְצָרִים
וְהוֹדֵה לַגְּבִיר כִּי הֶחֱשִׁיכָךְ
בְּאוֹרָה הַמְעֻלָּה כַּמְּאוֹרִים
אֲשֶׁר שָׂח כָּל־הֲדַר מֶלֶךְ לְפָנָיו
וְהָיוּ מַעֲלוֹת כָּל־שָׂר חֲסֵרִים
אֲשֶׁר בּוֹ יִמְלְכוּ כָל־הַמְּלָכִים
וּבוֹ מִתְיָעֲצִים רֹזְנִים וְשָׂרִים
הֲקִימוּהוּ כְּמוֹ מַלְכָּם וְהָיָה
כְּפִיר בָּהֶם וְכֻלָּם הַשְּׁוָרִים
מְנַהֵל צֹאן עֲלֵי מִרְעֶה אֱמוּנוֹת
וְלֹא נֶעְדַּר מְאוּמָה מֵעֲדָרִים
וְהוּא בָהֶם כְּמַלְאַךְ הָאֱלֹהִים
בְּעֵת לֹא מָצְאוּ מֵאֵל דְּבָרִים
יְקַר נֶפֶשׁ עֲדֵי שַׁחַק נְדִיב לֵב
בְּלִי יָדֹר יְשַׁלֵּם הַנְּדָרִים
אֲשֶׁר לֹא כָהֲתָה עֵינוֹ בְמַתָּן
וְלֹא עָצַר כְּמַתַּן הַמְּטָרִים
אֲשֶׁר מָלְיוּ בְּמִפְעָלָיו קְשׁוּרִים
כְּרָאשִׁים נִקְשְׁרוּ בָהֶם כְּתָרִים

boasting that they were the best of all

    because they are like young deer.

But when the sun rose over them,

    I cried out, "Halt! Do not cross the boundaries!

Admit that our noble lord eclipses you,

    with light as bright as any sun!

No king seems glorious before him,

    and no grandee seems great.

Through him the potent rule; from him

    all princes and all lords get counsel.

They raise him up as if he were their king;

    he a lion, they the oxen.

He guides the sheep to quiet pasture;

    not one among his flock gets lost.

He is an angel of the Lord to them,

    when they themselves can find no word from God.

Proud ornament of heaven, so generous

    he doesn't deign to pledge; he simply gives.

His eye is never dimmed by gifts,

    nor does he dry up like the gift of rain.

His words befit his deeds

    as crowns match heads.

וְכָל־הָרְזָנִים אֵלָיו יְסוּרוּן
וְכַיָּם נִמְשְׁכוּ אֵלָיו נְהָרִים
וְאָמְנָם הוּא כְּרֹאשׁ עַל הָאֲדָמָה
וְהוּא אֶחָד כְּנֶגֶד הַיְצוּרִים.

Rulers come to pay him court,

    as rivers flow toward the ocean.

In sum: he is a head above the earth.

    Alone, he counterbalances all creatures."

אֲדֹנִי קַח בְּכַפְּךָ מְתוּקָה
וְתָרִיחַ וְתִשְׁכַּח הַתְּשׁוּקָה
אֲדַמְדֶּמֶת שְׁתֵּי פָנִים כְּכַלָּה
בְּבֹא רֵאשִׁית שְׁתֵּי יָדַי בְּחֵיקָהּ
יְתוֹמָה הִיא וְאֵין לָהּ אָב וְאָחוֹת
וְגַם מֵעַל אֲמִירֶיהָ רְחוֹקָה
וְעֵת שֶׁנִּלְקְחָה חָמְדוּ חֲבֵרוֹת
הֲלִיכָתָהּ וְצָעֲקוּ לָהּ צְעָקָה
שְׂאִי שָׁלוֹם לְרַב יִצְחָק אֲדֹנֵךְ
וְאַשְׁרֵךְ שֶׁבְּפִיו תִּהְיִי נְשׁוּקָה.

MASTER, TAKE this thing of sweetness in your hand,

    sniff it, and your pining goes away.

Before men's gaze, it blushes like a bride

    when first her husband reaches for her breast.

An orphan, with no father and no sister,

    far away from her familiar boughs.

When she was picked for you, her apple girlfriends

    envied her for leaving, and they cried:

"Give our love to Master Isaac, your new lord.

    Lucky apple, to be kissed by him!"

הֲיֵשׁ כָּזֹאת בְּצֶמַח הָאֲדָמָה
סָגֹר מִחוּץ וְכֶסֶף מִפְּנִימָה
רְאִינוּהָ וְלִבְנָתָהּ כְּאִלּוּ
בְּעֵינֵינוּ יְעַטְּנוּהָ כְלִמָּה
כְּעַלְמָה שֶׁרְדָפוּהָ אֲנָשִׁים
וְנֶהֶפְכָה לְרֹב בָּשְׁתָּהּ אֲדָמָּה.

IS THERE ANOTHER fruit like this?—

    Gold outside, and on the inside silver!

We noticed it was white, as if

    embarrassed by our staring,

as if it were a girl whom men

    were chasing and who blushed for shame.

אֶכֹל גִּזְרָה מְשַׂחֶקֶת
כְּמוֹ בָרָק וּבָרָקֶת
אֲשֶׁר תֵּרָא אֲדָמָּה עֵת
וְעֵת אַחֵר יְרַקְרָקֶת
וְתִתְהַפֵּךְ כְּמוֹ חוֹלָה
בְּיֵרָקוֹן וְדַלֶּקֶת
כְּאִלּוּ הִיא גְּלִיל כֶּסֶף
בְּזָהָב טוֹב מְחָשֶּׁקֶת
תְּמַהּ כִּי לֹא יָדְעָה אִישׁ
וְשָׁדֶיהָ כְּמֵינֶקֶת
וּבִרְצוֹת שִׁלְפֵי חֶרֶב
לְהַכּוֹתָהּ בְּמַפְרָקֶת
אֲזַי תִּפֹּל לְרַגְלֵיהֶם
וְשִׂפְתֵיהֶם מְנַשֶּׁקֶת.

BITE INTO THIS smiling thing
    that looks like lightning or topaz.
Sometimes you might think it's red,
    sometimes you might call it greenish.
Turn it, and it's like a girl,
    sick with jaundice or with fever.
Or maybe it's a silver sphere
    with a hoop of finest gold.
Strange: a virgin, but her breast
    is round as any nursing mother's.
If fighter draws his sword,
    draws and strikes her on her neck—
at his feet she falls, but later
    kisses him upon the lips.

הֲלֹא תִרְאוּ חֲבַצֶּלֶת
אֲשֶׁר גּוּפָהּ כְּמַלְבּוּשָׁהּ
אֲשֶׁר תֵּבוֹשׁ לְכָל־עַיִן
כְּכַלָּה מִפְּנֵי אִישָׁהּ
וְכִבְתוּלָה מְשַׂחֶקֶת
וְיָדֶיהָ עֲלֵי רֹאשָׁהּ.

BEHOLD the rose:
Her body's like her garment.
When you look at her, she blushes
like a bride before her husband,
or like a girl who runs out screaming,
her hands upon her head in horror.

קָרָא הַצִּיר עָלַי אֲחִי שְׁלוֹמוֹת
אֲשֶׁר נֶעְדָּר כְּמוֹתוֹ בָּאֲדָמוֹת
אֲשֶׁר הִזְכִּיר וְלֹא יִשְׁכַּח לְבָבִי
בְּעוֹד חַי מַתְּנוֹתָיו הָעֲצוּמוֹת
בְּשָׁלְחוֹ כַף מְלֵאָה מִבְּשָׂמִים
יְמַלֵּא אֵל בְּיָדוֹ הַנְּעִימוֹת
אֲשֶׁר בָּהּ כָּל־יְרַקְרֶקֶת דְּמוּתָהּ
כְּחוֹלָה כָּתֳנֹתֶיהָ פְּרֻמוֹת
אֲדָמוֹת נֶאֱחַז מֵהֶן לְעֵין אִישׁ
אֲשֶׁר נֶאֱחַז לְלִבּוֹ מֵחֲלוֹמוֹת
גְּוִיָּתָן אֲדֻמָּה תּוֹךְ לְבוּשָׁן
לְאֶרֶץ שֶׁסְּבִיבָהּ חֵל וְחוֹמוֹת
וּבֶן שַׁחַק אֲשֶׁר אָבִיו הֲדָפוֹ
וְנֶאֱסַף בַּלְּחִי בֹּשֶׁת וְאֵימוֹת
וּמֵהֶן שֶׁיְּדָעָן אִישׁ וּמֵהֶן
אֲשֶׁר לֹא נוֹדְעוּ וָהֵן סְתֻמוֹת
אֲשֶׁר כָּסּוּ צְעִיפֵי שֵׁשׁ פְּנֵיהֶן
כְּנָשִׁים מֵאֲנָשִׁים נַעֲלָמוֹת
וְיֵרָאוֹן בְּהָסִיר הַצְּעִיפִים
לְאִישׁ חֵמָה אֲשֶׁר יִקַּח נְקָמוֹת

SPEAK, MESSENGER, my greetings to my friend,
     a man whose like does not exist on earth,
whose wondrous gifts my heart will ever praise
     and not forget as long as it may live.
He sent a salver full of fragrant flowers
     (so may his hands be filled with all delights!)—
greenish-yellow things, each like
     a sickly woman with her tunic torn;
red things that the eye perceives
     as much of as the heart perceives in dreams.
Inside their clothes, their bodies seem to me
     like a land inside concentric walls,
or like a laughing child whose father slaps him,
     coloring his cheeks with shame and fear.
Some have known men, others not,
     but still are sealed.
Their faces are concealed by linen veils,
     as women are concealed from men,
but when they take their veils off, they appear
     to a choleric and vengeful man

וְאַפֵּיהֶן כְּאִלּוּ פָשְׁעוּ בוֹ

וְהֵם לֹא פָשְׁעוּ מָלְאוּ כְלִמּוֹת

וְיֵרָא מִפְּנֵיהֶם אוֹר כְּאוֹר צַח

בְּעֵת שֶׁמַּרְכְּבוֹת יָמִים רְתוּמוֹת

וְיֵרָאוּ נִפְלָאוֹת חָכְמָה וּבִינָה

לְרֹאֵימוֹ וְאֵינֵימוֹ חֲכָמוֹת

כְּאִלּוּ עֵין אֱנוֹשׁ בִּרְאוֹת הַדָּרָן

לְבַב שָׂר שֶׁאֲפָפוּהוּ מְזִמּוֹת

וְכִלְבַב אִישׁ מְפַחֵד מֵחֲלוֹם אוֹ

כְּנֹפְלִים יַחֲלוּ לִמְצֹא תְקוּמוֹת

וְכָעַיִט אֲשֶׁר נִבְהַל בְּתוֹךְ פַּח

וְכַתַּלְמִיד בְּמַסֶּכֶת יְבָמוֹת

וְאֶדְעֵם בְּשׁוּרֵי הוֹד דְּמוּתָם

וְלֹא אוּכַל לְסַפֵּר אוֹ לְדַמּוֹת

כְּאִישִׁים שֶׁיְּדַעְתִּימוֹ בְּצוּרָם

אֲבָל לֹא נִקְבוּ עִמִּי בְּשֵׁמוֹת

וּבָרָא הַזְּמָן גֶּם יְרַקְרַק

וַיִּצֶר כָּתְנֹתֵיהֶם אֲדֻמּוֹת

וּמֵהֶם יַעֲלֶה לַהַט כְּאִלּוּ

בְּתוֹלַעַת וְאַרְגָּמָן קְרוּמוֹת

as if they had betrayed him—but they never did!—
    their faces red with shame.
From their faces shines a light like sunlight,
    when the chariots of day are hitched,
revealing wisdom's wonders to the watcher,
    though they have no wisdom of their own.
Contemplating them, a person's heart
    is like a courtier engulfed in plots,
like a man in panic from a dream,
    like people who have tripped and cannot rise,
like a vulture that has lurched into a trap,
    or like a student all bewildered
    by the laws of consanguinity.
I take their beauty in, I feel I know them,
    but I can't describe that beauty—
    even figurative language fails me.
They seem, by looks, like men I used to know,
    but whose names escape me.
Time has turned their bodies greenish-yellow,
    made their tunics red,
and they emit a glow as if a violet
    or scarlet membrane covered them.

וְאָכַל הַזְּמַן עוֹרָם עֲדֵי דַק
וְכִלָּה מִבְּשָׂרָם הָעֲצָמוֹת
וְנָבַר מִבְּלִי פֶּצַע בְּשָׂרָם
כְּמוֹ נֶפֶשׁ נְבָרָה מֵאֲשָׁמוֹת
וְהִרְחִיף בַּעֲדָם רֵיחַ בְּשָׂמִים
וְאָרַג בָּם עֲנַן קַיִץ רְקָמוֹת
יְבוּשׁוּן מִכְּלוֹת עֵין אִישׁ אֲלֵיהֶם
וְיָנִדוּ לְאַנְחַת הַנְּשָׁמוֹת
וְנֶפֶשׁ הָאֱנוֹשׁ תִּשְׂמַח בְּרֵיחָם
כְּלֵב חָכָם בְּמָצְאוֹ תַעֲלָמוֹת
וְאָמְנָם לוּ יְהוּשְׁמוּ עָלֵי אַף
נְדוּד שֵׁנָה אֲזַי שָׁכַח תְּנוּמוֹת
וְאִלּוּ נִתְּנוּ לַמֵּת לְקָחָם
וְשָׂמַח בָּאָרוֹן בָּם אַחֲרֵי מוֹת
וְלוּ בָאוּ לְבֵית הַגֵּא לְהוֹד תָּ—
אָדָם לֹא נִכְּרוּ מֵהָעֲלָמוֹת
בְּחָרוּם מֵעֲרוּגַת גַּן וּבָאוּ
בְּלִי רֶגֶל וְשׁוֹקֵיהֶן צְנָמוֹת
וְעֵת כִּי שְׁלָחָם הַשַּׂר לְפָנַי
חֲשַׁבְתִּים אֶגְרוֹת מֶלֶךְ חֲתוּמוֹת
בְּעֵת הִתְפָּרְקוּ יַחַד עֲלֵי כַף
וְגַם הִתְבּוֹלֲלוּ בָהּ כַּעֲרֵמוֹת

Time has consumed and thinned their skin

    and then consumed the bones beneath the flesh.

It gnawed their flesh but left no blemish,

    left them like a soul that's innocent of sin.

It wafted over them sweet fragrances.

    The summer cloud wove colors into them.

They feel ashamed when men's eyes long for them,

    and yet they sympathize with sighing souls.

Their scent delights the human soul

    as insight into mysteries

    delights philosophers.

Just put them on the nose of an insomniac,

    and he'll forget about his sleep.

Give them to a corpse; he'll grab them

    and enjoy them in his coffin after death.

Put them in Ahasuerus's harem:

    you couldn't tell them from the concubines.

Cut from their garden bed they came to us

    with scrawny thighs and footless.

When the master had them brought to me,

    I thought that they were royal letters under seal.

Unpacked and strewn upon a tray,

    jumbled on it, heaps on heaps,

כְּאִלּוּ קֻנְּאוּ אַחַת לְאַחַת

וְהֻגְּשׁוּ לְפָנַי הָעֲצָמוֹת

כְּלִילוֹת הוֹד וְיֹפִי לֹא חֲסֵרוֹת

מְאוּם וּכְמִפְעֲלוֹתֶיךָ שְׁלֵמוֹת

תְּמִימוֹת כַּאֲשֶׁר הוּא תָם לְבָבְךָ

וְנָבָר מִבְּלִי עוֹלוֹת וּמִרְמוֹת

מְעִידוֹת כִּי לְיָדְךָ הַנְּשׂוּאָה

בְּרוֹם עִם כּוֹכְבֵי שַׁחַק תְּשׂוּמוֹת

וְיָכוּ מַעֲלוֹתֶיךָ לְחַיֵּי

בְנוֹת יָמִים וְתִהְיֶינָה כְתֻמּוֹת

יְמַלֵּא עִמְּךָ הָאֵל חֲסָדָיו

וְיַרְבֶּה עִמְּךָ גְּבִישׁ וְרָאמוֹת

וְיַשְׁמִיד מִמְּךָ עָרִים וְיָרִים

מְקוֹמְךָ אֵל עֲלֵי כָל־הַמְּקֹמוֹת.

they seemed like women jealous of each other,

    bringing their dispute to me.

Perfect in their beauty, lacking nothing,

    perfect just like everything you do,

perfect, as your heart is perfect;

    pure, without transgression or deceit.

They testify that your uplifted hand

    has a stake among the stars of heaven.

May your excellences strike

    Days' daughters' cheeks and leave them stained.

May God bestow full favors on you,

    give you much of crystal and brocade,

destroy your enemies and elevate

    your place above all other stations.

רְאֵה שֶׁמֶשׁ לְעֵת עֶרֶב אֲדֻמָּה

כְּאִלּוּ לָבְשָׁה תוֹלָע לְמִכְסֶה

תְּפַשֵּׁט פַּאֲתֵי צָפוֹן וְיָמִין

וְרוּחַ יָם בְּאַרְגָּמָן תְּכַסֶּה

וְאֶרֶץ עָזְבָה אוֹתָהּ עֲרֻמָּה

בְּצֵל הַלַּיְלָה תָּלִין וְתֶחְסֶה

וְהַשַּׁחַק אֲזַי קָדַר כְּאִלּוּ

בְּשַׂק עַל מוֹת יְקוּתִיאֵל מְכַסֶּה.

BEHOLD THE SUN at evening, red
    as if she wore vermilion robes.
She slips the wraps from north and south,
    dresses the west in a purple gown,
then strips the earth and leaves it bare
    to shelter in shadows through the night.
At once the sky is black, as if
    in sackcloth for Yekutiel.

הֲלֹא תִרְאֶה מְיֻדָּעִי
שְׁחָקִים כַּעֲרוּגַת גַּן
וְכוֹכָבִים כְּשׁוֹשַׁנִּים
וְהַסַּהַר כְּמוֹ אַגָּן.

CAN YOU SEE what I see, friend?
The sky is like a garden bed.
The stars are flowers blooming there,
watered by a pool, the moon.

וְאָלִין וַאֲנִי נִבְהָל כְּאִלּוּ

שְׁנַת עֵינַי עֲלֵי עֵינַי אֲסוּרָה

וְהַשַּׁחַק כְּאֹהֶל בַּחֲבָלָיו

אֲשֶׁר הַלַּיְלָה בָהֶם קְשׁוּרָה

וּמַרְאֵה הַלְּבָנָה בַעֲיָשָׁהּ

כְּכַלָּה נַעֲרוֹתֶיהָ מְאִירָה

כְּאַיֶּלֶת סְבָבוּהָ צְבָאִים

אֲשֶׁר הַלַּיְלָה לָהֶם כְּפִירָה

וְהַכִּימָה בְּכוֹכָבִים אֲגוּדָה

כְּנֵרוֹת הֶעֱלוּ עַל הַמְּנוֹרָה

וְרֹאשׁ הַלַּיְלָה כָּפַף בְּשֵׂיבוֹ

כְּבֶן שִׁשִּׁים וְעֶשְׂרִים וַעֲשָׂרָה

וְהִנֵּה כוֹכְבֵי שַׁחַק לְנֶגְדִּי

כְּרָצִים שֶׁאֱלִים קַחַת בְּשׂוֹרָה

I SPENT the night in agitation. It seemed as if
    my eyes had been enjoined from sleeping.
The sky was like a tent with ropes
    that kept the night attached to it.
The moon alongside heaven's Bear
    was like a beaming bride among her maidens,
or like a doe surrounded by a herd of bucks,
    all threatened by the night, a lion.
The Pleiades, a little knot of stars,
    were like the lights upon a candle stand.
Night's head, with its white hair, was stooped
    as if it were a ninety-year-old man.
Suddenly, the heaven's stars appeared to me
    like runners eager to deliver tidings.

יְדִידִי נַהֲלֵנִי עַל גְּפָנִים
וְהַשְׁקֵנִי וְאִמָּלֵא שִׂשׂוֹנִים
וְכוֹסוֹת אַהֲבָתְךָ יִדְבְּקוּ בִי
וְאוּלַי הֵם יְנִיסוּן הַיָּגוֹנִים
וְאִם תִּשְׁתֶּה בְּאַהֲבָתִי שְׁמֹנֶה
אֲנִי אֶשְׁתֶּה בְּאַהֲבָתְךָ שְׁמֹנִים

וְאִם אָמוּת לְפָנֶיךָ יְדִידִי
חֲצֹב קִבְרִי בְּשָׁרְשֵׁי הַגְּפָנִים
וְשִׂים רַחְצִי בְּמֵימֵי הָעֲנָבִים
וְחָנְטֵנִי בְּחַרְצַנִּים וְזַגִּים
וְאַל תִּבְכֶּה וְאַל תָּנוּד לְמוֹתִי
עֲשֵׂה כִנּוֹר וְעוּגָבִים וּמִנִּים
וְאַל תָּשִׂים עֲלֵי קִבְרִי עֲפָרִים
אֲבָל כַּדִּים חֲדָשִׁים עִם יְשָׁנִים.

BRING ME to the vineyard, friend.

    Give me a drink, and pour me full of joy.

Keep your cups of friendship close to me—

    maybe they will drive away my sorrow.

Hoist the cup eight times to me,

    and I'll drink eighty times to you.

If you see me dying there,

    dig my grave among the vines.

Wash my corpse with must of grapes.

    Embalm me with the pips and skins.

Do not weep and do not mourn,

    but work the lute, the harp, the lyre.

Don't fill in my grave with dirt—

    only wine-jugs, old and new.

וְאַל תִּתְמַהּ וְאַל יָרוּם לְבָבֶךְ
לְמַעַן כִּי תְחִלָּה בָּאֲשִׁישׁוֹת.
וְחָכְמָתְךָ לְרַפֵּא הַגְּוִיּוֹת
וְחָכְמָתִי לְרַפֵּא הַנְּפָשׁוֹת.

DON'T BE self-satisfied or vain
  that people clamor for your wine.
Your craft is healing people's bodies—
  healing people's souls is mine.

שְׂפַת מִזְרָק מְנַשֶּׁקֶת שְׂפָתִי
כְּשֶׁמֶשׁ זָרְחָה עַל כַּף עֲמִיתִי
בְּמֵימֵי הַגְּפָנִים בָּעֲרָה אֵשׁ
וְתֹאכְלֵנִי וְלֹא תֹאכַל כְּסוּתִי
וְעוֹד לֹא רָאֲתָה עַיִן כְּמַרְאֶה
זְכוֹכִית יַעֲשֶׂה אָדָם דְּמוּתִי
אֲשֶׁר בַּלָּט יְדַבֵּר לִי עֲסִיסוֹ
חֲדַל טֶרֶם יְבַעְתְּךָ שְׂאֵתִי
וְאֵיכָה תַעַרֹךְ שֶׁמֶשׁ לְאוֹרִי
וְלִי יִתְרוֹן עֲלֵי שֶׁמֶשׁ כְּצֵאתִי
לְמַעַן כִּי גְוִיָּתָהּ עֲרֻמָּה
וְהַסַּפִּיר וְהַשֹּׁהַם כְּסוּתִי
וְאֵיךְ תַּשְׁוֶה דְבָרַי הַמְהֻלָּל
לְאִישׁ גָּזַל מְעַט מִתַּאֲוָתִי

שְׁתִינוּהוּ וְהַבָּרָק מְפַזֵּז
לְגָרֵשׁ הָאֲפֵלָה מִנְּוָתִי
יְפַזֵּר בַּעֲדָהּ תַּרְשִׁישׁ וּבָרֶקֶת
וְיָפִין בָּאֲפָסֶיהָ שְׁנָתִי

THE GOBLET'S LIP that kisses mine

    gleams like a sun in my comrade's hand.

Within the vine's juice burns a flame—

    a flame consuming me but not my clothing.

The eye has never yet beheld a crystal cup

    that made a man who looks like me,

a cup of wine that whispers in my ear,

    "Let me alone, before I rise and stun you!

How do you dare compare me to the sun,

    when I rise mightier than he,

when he is just a naked body

    and I wear crystal raiment?

How can you compare my glorious self

    to one whose glamour is purloined from me?"

We were drinking wine while lightning danced,

    banishing the darkness from my home

by strewing it with jaspers and with sapphires,

    and scattering afar all thought of sleep.

וְיִתְפָּאֵר בְּפַח זָהָב עֲלֵי עָב

תְּלַקֵּט שַׁרְשְׁרוֹת זָהָב בְּבֵיתִי

וּמֵימֶיהָ כְּמוֹ שֶׁלֶג שְׂנִיר אוֹ

כְּמוֹ שִׁירַת שְׁמוּאֵל הַקְּהָתִי.

It boasted of its sheets of gold, competing with the cloud
  that gets its golden necklace from my house.
The rain was cold as snow on Mount Hermon, as cold
  as Samuel the Nagid's poetry.

בָּרָק אֲשֶׁר עֵינוֹ כְּעֵין בָּרֶקֶת
שֶׁלְחָה לְגַנַּת הַהֲדַס מֵינָקֶת
וּפָקַד עֲרוּגַת הַבְּשָׂמִים וְאֶסֹר
הֶעָב לְבִלְתִּי תִהְיֶה נִתָּקֶת
בָּרָק בָּרֹק אֶל הַהֲדַס כִּי שָׁחֲחָה
וַתַּעֲמֹד מִנֶּגְדְּךָ דְּפָקֶת

עָב לַעֲבֹר לֹא אִוְּתָה עַד רֻוְּתָה
נֶפֶשׁ עֲרוּגָה הָיְתָה שֹׁקֶקֶת
רְאֵה לְבָבִי נִפְלָאוֹת שַׁדַּי בְּשׁוּר
הֶעָב אֲשֶׁר תִּבְכֶּה וְהִיא שׂחָקֶת
תִּזְרֹק רְסִיסֶיהָ בְּיַד חָרוּץ כְּמוֹ
יַד אַהֲרֹן עַל מִזְבְּחוֹ זֹרֶקֶת
תִּתֵּן בְּנִצָּיָהּ כְּתֹבֶת קַעֲקַע
וּבְמִשְׁבְּצוֹת כַּרְמִיל וּבוּץ חֲקֻקֶת
קִטֵּר שְׂדֵה בֹשֶׂם קְטֹרֶת מֹר לְמוּל
עָנָן אֲשֶׁר נִבְקַע וְרֶץ לְצָקֶת
בִּרְאוֹת צְמָאָיו אָמְרוּ כָּסוּ וְלֹא
כָּסוּ בְּיֵרָקוֹן וְלֹא דָלָקֶת

JASPER-COLORED lightning, send
　　a cloud as wet-nurse to the myrtle garden.
Tend the flower bed and bind
　　that cloud so that it can't get free.
Flash, lightning, toward that myrtle bush;
　　she stands before you bowed and dripping.

The cloud refused to move along until
　　it satisfied the garden's thirsty soul.
My heart observed a miracle of God:
　　the garden laughing as the cloud wept,
sprinkling droplets with an eager hand,
　　as Aaron used to sprinkle blood upon his altar,
tattooing the garden with her buds,
　　inscribing colored patches, red and white.
The flower-field burned myrrh as incense
　　to the cloud, which quickly burst and poured.
Whoever saw its plants exclaimed,
　　"It's covered"—but it wasn't—
　　"with sickly blight and fever-red."

לוּ אֹהֲבֵי נַפְשִׁי אֲמַתְּכֶם תֶּחֱזוּ

בֵּין צִלְלֵי כָל־עֵץ פְּרִי נֶאֱקֶת

אִם אֶגְוְעָה מִשְּׂאֵת יְגוֹנִים נֶגְדְּכֶם

כַּסּוּ עֲצָמַי בַּעֲצֵי שָׂדָקֶת

לִמְיַסְּרֶיךָ אַל תְּנַעֵר חָצְנְךָ

כִּי בָאֱהָבִים נַפְשְׁךָ דְּבָקֶת

הִנֵּה בְשׁוּט אוֹר יַעֲלַת הַחֵן בְּךָ

לוּ דִבְּרָה עוֹד נִשְׁבְּרָה מַפְרָקֶת

אַל תִּזְכְּרוּ אַל תִּזְכְּרוּ הָאַהֲבָה

כִּי אַהֲבַת נַעַר כְּאֵשׁ נִשְׁקֶת.

If only, friends, you saw my soul, your concubine,
        moaning amid the shade of all the fruit trees!
If you should see me die of sorrows borne,
        cover up my bones with the finest vines.
"Don't shake off people who berate you
        because you're love-addicted!
When that beauty's light flits by you—
        if she would speak to you,
        you'd tip back, break your neck."
"Don't speak of—no, don't speak of love,
        for youthful love is like a burning fire!"

אֱהִי פִדְיוֹן לְעֹפֶר הָאֲהָבִים
אֲשֶׁר בּוֹ כָּל־מְתֵי יָגוֹן שְׂמֵחִים
אֲשֶׁר יִדְמוּ לְאַבְנֵי שֵׁשׁ לְחָיָיו
כְּאִלּוּ הֵם בְּדַם חֵשֶׁק מְשָׁחִים
וְנִיבָיו מִשְׂפָּתָיו כַּשְּׁלָחִים
וְעֵינָיו בַּלְּבָבוֹת כָּרְמָחִים.

THAT FAWN of love! I'd sell my soul for him.

    The sight of him cheers even brooding men.

His cheeks are white and red, like marble slabs

    all smeared with lovers' blood.

His teeth are lances ranged behind his lips. His eyes

    transfix his lovers' hearts like spears.

תְּנָה הַכּוֹס וְאִם אֵין שְׁתֵהוּ
וְכִדְמוּת לְחָיֶךְ הַכַּד רְאֵהוּ
וְחִלָּה מִמְּךָ כִּמְעַט וְיָמוּת
בְּעֵינַיִם כְּחוֹלִים הַחֲיֵהוּ
מְשָׁל־בָּנוּ בְּמִצְוַת דָּר עֲרָבוֹת
וְאִם בִּלְבָבְךָ צֶדֶק עֲשֵׂהוּ.

PASS THE CUP, or take a drink yourself,

and note the way the cup reflects your cheek.

Here's a sick man like to die for you.

Revive him with those languid eyes of yours.

Dominate us as the Lord commands,

And if there's any good in you, just do it.

יְשׁוּרֵנִי וְעַפְעַפָּיו כְּחֹלָה
וְהַכּוֹס מִדְּמוֹת לֶחְיוֹ מְמֻלָּה
וְנִיבָיו מִשְׁפָּתָיו דַּר עֲלֵי דַר
וּבִשְׂחוֹק פִּיו בְּכֶתֶם לֹא יְסֻלֶּה
וְהַנִּיבוֹת אֲשֶׁר בָּם יִקְטְלֵנִי
כְּנִיב נֹשֶׁה עֲלֵי אִישׁ רָשׁ וְנִקְלֶה
וְהַכּוֹס רָץ כְּשֶׁמֶשׁ בַּשְּׁחָקִים
וְהַיּוֹם נָד נְדֹד רֵעִים וְגֹלֶה
וְדָמִי יַעֲרֹךְ עֲלֵי וְנִבְהָל
עֲלֵי לֶחְיִי וְלֹא יֵרַד וְעֹלֶה.

HE EYES ME: eyelids like an invalid's.

    His cheeks' reflection fills the cup.

Behind his lips, his teeth are pearl on pearl.

    That smile of his outweighs the finest gold.

The words he speaks to me are deadly words,

    like a creditor who duns a pauper.

The cup goes round like the sun in the sky.

    The day departs. So friends disappear.

My blood is raining all over me, rushing

    down on my cheek, to go up no more.

כְּתָמָר אַתְּ בְּקוֹמָתֵךְ
וְכַשֶּׁמֶשׁ בְּיָפְיָתֵךְ
חֲשַׁבְתִּיךְ בַּעֲלַת צֶדֶק
אֲבִיגַיִל בְּצִדְקָתֵךְ
מְצָאתִיךְ כִּי הֲרַגְתְּנִי
כְּאִיזֶבֶל בְּרִשְׁעָתֵךְ

כְּלִילַת הוֹד יְפַת מַרְאֶה
אֲנִי חֹלֶה בְּאַהֲבָתֵךְ
וְהַעֲלִי מִשְּׁאוֹל נַפְשִׁי
וְאַל אָמוּת לְעֻמָּתֵךְ.

LOFTY AS a palm tree,
     luminous as the sun!
I assumed that you were good,
     an Abigail for loyalty,
and then I found you killing me,
     wicked as a Jezebel.

Perfect beauty, lovely face!
     I'm failing, out of love for you.
Snatch me from the pit of doom.
     Don't stand there watching as I die.

נַפְשִׁי בְּמִסְתָּרִים תִּבְכֶּה עֲלֵי גֵוָה

שֶׁצָּף בְּשֶׁצֶף הַחִבָּה וְהַתַּאֲוָה

כַּמָּה יְיַחֵל אִישׁ כָּלֶה אֲשֶׁר גּוּפוֹ

כָּלָה וְאֵין תּוֹחֶלֶת לוֹ וְלֹא תִקְוָה

לוּ תִשְׁקְלוּהוּ עִם הֶבֶל אֲשֶׁר נִשְׁוֶה

גּוּף נֶחֱלָה עִם נֶפֶשׁ כָּלְתָה דָוָה

הַשְׁכְּנִי מָרוֹם לָמָּה בְרָאתַנִי

לָמָּה הֲרֹג עַיִן מִכָּל־בְּנֵי עַלְוָה.

MY SOUL laments its body secretly,
 swept away in floods of love and passion.
How long, the longing of a mortal man,
 whose body perishes, whose hope is gone,
who weighs no more than air, whose sickly body
 balances a sickly soul?
O God on high! Why did You ever make me,
 a man destroyed by every haughty eye? O why?

אַמְנוֹן אֲנִי חֲלֵה קִרְאוּ אֱלֵי תָמָר

כִּי חֶשְׁקָה נָפַל בְּרֶשֶׁת וְגַם מִכְמָר

רֵעַי מְיֻדָּעַי אֵלַי הֲבָאוּהָ

אַחַת שְׁאֵלָתִי מִכֶּם אֲשֶׁר אֹמַר

קִשְׁרוּ עֲטֶרֶת עַל רֹאשָׁהּ וְהָכִינוּ

עֶדְיָהּ וְשִׂימוּ עַל יָדָהּ בְּכוֹס חָמָר

תָּבֹא וְתַשְׁקֵנִי אוּלַי תְּכַבֶּה אֵשׁ

לִבִּי אֲשֶׁר בָּלָה בְּשָׂרִי אֲשֶׁר סָמָר.

I AM SICK, like Amnon. Call Tamar,

    and say that death has nearly snared a man who loves her.

Friends, companions! Bring her here to me—

    that's the only thing I ask of you.

Crown her, make her wear her jewelry,

    and send along with her a cup of wine.

Maybe if she'd pour for me, she would put out

    the burning pain that wastes my throbbing flesh.

Devotional Poems

בַּעֲלוֹת יָהּ עַל לְבָבִי
כִּי בְכֹל אֵין לָךְ דְּמוּת אֵין
זִכְרְךָ תַּבַּע שְׂפָתִי
אִם הֲשַׁכְתִּיהָ תִּמְאַן.

WHEN THE THOUGHT of God comes to my mind
(for nothing, nothing in the All resembles You),
my lips and tongue pronounce Your Holy Name;
I couldn't stop them if I wanted to.

אֲשֶׁר רָאָה לְכָל־צָפוּן וְחָזָה
וְלֹא שִׁקֵּץ עֱנוּת עָנִי וּבֵזָה
לְהָבִין דַּעְתְּךָ הַרְחֵב לְבָבִי
וְשִׂימָה־נָא לְעַבְדְּךָ בָּהּ אֲחֻזָּה
וְאָז אֶשְׂבַּע תְּמוּנָתְךָ בְּהָקִיץ
וְתַחַת כִּסְאֲךָ נַפְשִׁי גְנוּזָה

O YOU WHO SEES all hidden things,

 Who would not scorn a sufferer:

Expand my heart to know Your mind,

 and grant this slave a share therein,

that I may lodge beneath Your throne,

 and while awake, behold Your face.

אֱלֹהַי שָׂא עֲוֹנוֹתַי וְכַפֵּר

וְאִם עָצְמוּ וְרַבּוּ מִלְסַפֵּר

וְזָכְרָה לִי חֲסָדֶיךָ יְיָ

וְאַל תִּפְקֹד עֲוֺן עָפָר וָאֵפֶר

וְאִם יָצְאָה גְזֵרָה לַהֲמִיתִי

אֱלֹהַי בַּטְּלָה אוֹתָהּ וְהָפֵר

וְשִׂימָה־נָּא פְדוּתִי מַחֲלָתִי

וְתוּגָתִי מְקוֹם מוֹתִי וְכֻפֵּר.

O LORD, EFFACE my sins and wipe them clean,

    though they be terrible, uncountable.

Keep me in mind for grace, O Lord;

    put out of mind the sins of dust and ashes.

If death is Your decree for me, O Lord,

    annul and cancel that decree, I pray.

Let this illness substitute for death,

    and let my sorrows be my expiation.

שָׁאַל לְהוֹדוֹת לָךְ לִבִּי וְלֹא יָכֹל

לוּ יֵשׁ תְּבוּנָתִי רָחְבָּה כְּמוֹ כַלְכֹּל

לְבִּי הֲלֹא טֶרֶם יַשְׂכִּיל פְּלָאֶיךָ

גָּדְלוּ חֲסָדֶיךָ עָלַי וְעַל הַכֹּל

מִבַּלְתְּךָ אֵין לִי מִבְטָח וְאַיֵּה צוּר

סוֹבֵל וְגַם תּוֹלֶה עוֹלָם כְּמוֹ אֶשְׁכֹּל

הֵן לָךְ אֲנִי נִשְׁלָךְ אֵיךְ לֹא אֲקַנֶּה־לָךְ

וּבְיָדְךָ נֶפֶשׁ כָּל־חַי וְרוּחַ כֹּל.

MY HEART would like to sing Your praise

      but could not do so properly,

      were I wise as any sage of old.

Before my mind could grasp Your miracles,

      Your favors overwhelmed me,

      as they overwhelm the world.

None is there to trust but You, You Who suspends

      the universe above the void

      as if it were a bunch of grapes.

Yes, You alone I trust. Could it be otherwise,

      when in Your hand is every creature's soul,

      and of the All besides?

שַׁדַּי אֲשֶׁר יַקְשִׁיב לַדַּל וְיֶעָתֵר

עַד אָן תְּהִי רָחוֹק מֶנִּי וְתִסָּתֵר

לַיִל וְיוֹם אֶעְטֹף אֶקְרָא בְּלֵב נָכוֹן

אוֹדֶה לְךָ תָּמִיד כִּי חַסְדְּךָ יָתֵר

מַלְכִּי לְךָ אוֹחִיל לִבִּי בְךָ יִבְטַח

כְּחוֹלֵם חֲלוֹם סָתוּם יִבְטַח עֲלֵי פוֹתֵר

הִנֵּה שְׁאֵלָתִי הַקְשֵׁב תְּחִנָּתִי

אוֹתָהּ אֲבַקֵּשׁ לֹא פָחוֹת וְלֹא יוֹתֵר.

ALMIGHTY ONE, Who hears a poor man's prayer—
How long will You keep hidden far from me?
I pray in sorrow day and night with loyal heart,
thanking You for Your abundant grace.
I place my hopes in You, O king, my heart secure,
like one who dreams a dream obscure,
trusting the interpreter.
So here is what I ask: Just hear my prayer.
I ask for nothing less, and nothing more.

שַׁתִּי בָךְ מַחְסִי בְּפַחְדִּי וְחֶרְדָּתִי
וּשְׁמָךְ בְּעֵת מָצוֹר שַׂמְתִּי מְצוּדָתִי
לִשְׂמֹאל וְעַל יָמִין אַבִּיט וְאֵין עוֹזֵר
כִּי אִם בְּיָדֶיךָ אַפְקִיד יְחִידָתִי
מִכָּל־יְקַר אֶרֶץ חֲלָקִי נָתַתִּיךְ
מִכָּל־עֲמָלִי אַתְּ חִשְׁקִי וְחֶמְדָּתִי
הִנֵּה בְּרֹב אַהֲבָה אֶשְׁגֶּה בָךְ תָּמִיד
עֵת תֵּת זְמִירוֹת לָךְ הָיְתָה עֲבוֹדָתִי.

IN ANXIETY, I go to You for refuge.

    Attacked, I make a fortress of Your Name.

If, peering left and right, I see no help,

    I give my soul in trust to You alone.

Of all the treasures of the world, I choose

    nothing but You, best-loved of all I have.

That love has kept You ever in my mind,

    above all, when my task is making songs.

טֶרֶם הֱיוֹתִי חַסְדְּךָ בָאֲנִי
הַשֵּׁם לְיֵשׁ אַיִן וְהִמְצִיאַנִי

מִי הוּא אֲשֶׁר רָקַם תְּמוּנָתִי וּמִי
עָצְמִי בְּכוּר יָצַק וְהִקְפִּיאַנִי
מִי הוּא אֲשֶׁר נָפַח נְשָׁמָה בִי וּמִי
בֶּטֶן שְׁאוֹל פָּתַח וְהוֹצִיאַנִי
מִי נִהֲגַנִי מִנְּעוּרַי עַד הֲלֹם
מִי לִמְּדַנִי בִין וְהִפְלִיאַנִי
אָמְנָם אֲנִי חֹמֶר בְּקֶרֶב יָדֶךָ
אַתָּה עֲשִׂיתַנִי אֱמֶת לֹא אֲנִי

אוֹדֶה עֲלֵי פִשְׁעִי וְלֹא אֹמַר לְךָ
כִּי הָעֲרִים נָחָשׁ וְהִשִּׁיאַנִי
אֵיכָה אֲכַחֵד מִמְּךָ חֶטְאִי הֲלֹא
טֶרֶם הֱיוֹתִי חַסְדְּךָ בָאֲנִי.

BEFORE I WAS, Your kindness came to me,
    when You made nothing be, creating me.

Who was it wove my form? Who poured
    and fired my matter in the kiln?
Who was it breathed the soul in me? Who opened
    Sheol's womb and let me go forth free?
Who guided me till now from infancy?
    Who gave me thought, my gift distinctively?
True, to You I never can be more than clay.
    True, You made me; never I made me.

I own my guilt. I do not say I strayed
    because some snake beguiled me craftily.
How could I hide my sin from You? For see:
    before I was, Your kindness came to me.

לְךָ אֵל חַי תִּכְסֹף יְחִידָתִי
וְגַם תִּכְלֶה רוּחִי וְנִשְׁמָתִי

שְׁכִינָתְךָ
שָׁכְנָה בְּתוֹךְ לִבּוֹת
סְגֻלָּתְךָ
בָּנִים וְגַם אָבוֹת
וְחַיָּתְךָ
לִרְתּוֹם בְּמֶרְכָּבוֹת
וּמָלֵאתִי זֹהַר בְּלִבָּתִי
מְנוֹרָתִי תָּאִיר לְעַמָּתִי

לְבַב מַשְׂכִּיל
יִלְאֶה לְהָבִין סוֹד
וְלֹא יָכִיל
לַחְקֹר תְּמוּנַת הוֹד
וְאֵיךְ אָכִיל
אֶת־מִמְּעוֹן כָּבוֹד
בְּאַוָּתִי אֶשָׁאַף לְיָקְרָתִי
כְּבוּדָּתִי אָשִׂים מְגַמָּתִי

TO YOU, O LIVING GOD, my soul is yearning,
my spirit and my life-breath languishing.

Your Presence dwells
within the hearts
of those You treasure—
sons and fathers
and Your angels,
who tend Your throne.
My heart is filled with radiance.
A lamp within me lights my way.

The wise man's mind
cannot grasp Your mystery,
or penetrate
Your splendor's form.
Yet inside me is a certain thing
from that same splendor's source!
Avidly aspiring for my precious one,
I make my object the beloved within:

מְעוֹן בִּינָה

עֶצֶם כְּמוֹ סַפִּיר

דְּמוּת לְבָנָה

כֶּתֶם זְהַב אוֹפִיר

וְהִיא שָׁכְנָה

מִסְתָּר בְּגוּף כִּכְפִיר

וְשִׂמְחָתִי גִילִי בְּאַנְחָתִי

וְשִׂיחָתִי וּצְנִיף מִזְמָתִי

הֲיוּכַל אִישׁ

הָתֵם לְמַהְלָלָהּ

וּמִי יַכְחִישׁ

יָפְיָהּ וּמַכְלוּלָהּ

עֲנֵה אֶל חִישׁ

בַּת אַהֲבָה חוֹלָה

לְאַט בִּתִּי מִמֵּי יְשׁוּעָתִי

הֲלֹא תִשְׁתִּי כִּי אַתְּ אֲיֻמָתִי.

Abode of wisdom,
substance crystalline,
moon-silver,
Ophir-gold,
lion crouching
in the body's covert,
my joy, my happiness in grief,
obsession, crown of all my thoughts.

Who can give her
the praise she's due?
Who denies
her beauty, her perfection?
Answer, Lord, and soon
that maiden sick with love.
"Patience, girl! In no time you will drink
my saving waters, you my own true love."

לְךָ נַפְשִׁי תְּסַפֵּר כִּי יְצַרְתָּהּ
וְתַגִּיד כִּי בְּיָדְךָ אֵל פְּעַלְתָּהּ
לְךָ בִּדְבַר יְהִי אָז נִמְצְאָה הִיא
וּמֵאַיִן כְּאוֹר עַיִן מְשַׁכְתָּהּ
לְךָ תַאֲמִין וְגַם תּוֹדֶה בְּיָמִין
וְתָעִיד כִּי בְקִרְבִּי אַתְּ נְפַחְתָּהּ
לְךָ תוֹדֶה עֲלֵי עֵדוּת בְּעֵדוּת
אֱמֶת כִּי לַעֲשׂוֹת חֶפְצָךְ שְׁלַחְתָּ
לְךָ אָמָה בְּעוֹדָהּ בָּאֲדָמָה
וְיוֹם תָּשׁוּב לְךָ כַּאֲשֶׁר נְתַתָּהּ
לְךָ עָצְמָה וְאַתָּה הוּא מְקוֹמָהּ
וְאַתְּ עִמָּהּ בְּכָל־קוּמָה וְשִׁבְתָּהּ
לְךָ מֵעֵת הֱיוֹתָהּ יֵשׁ חֲיוֹתָהּ
וּמִפִּיךָ תְּבוּנָתָהּ וְדַעְתָּהּ
לְךָ תִדְרֹשׁ דְּבַר חָקָּהּ וְשָׁפְקָהּ
לְךָ תוֹדֶה עֲלֵי מֵימָהּ וּפִתָּהּ
לְךָ תוֹחִיל בְּיוֹם תִּזְעַק וְתָחִיל
בְּרֹב צָרָהּ כְּמַבְכִּירָה בְלִדְתָּהּ

TO YOU MY SOUL attributes her creation,

>   attests that with Your hand You fashioned her.

At Your word "Be!" she came to be.

>   As light emerges from the pupil's black,

>   You drew her forth from nothingness.

To You she gives her trust. She lifts her arm and swears

>   that You it was Who breathed her into me.

To You she owns her servitude,

>   confesses that You sent her here to do Your will.

To You she is a servant here on earth

>   and after she returns to You as when You sent her forth.

To You belongs her essence. You are where she is.

>   You are with her, idle or in action.

To You the task of keeping her alive;

>   from You her wisdom and her intellect.

To You she goes to seek her sustenance.

>   To You she gives her thanks for bread and water.

To You she looks when crying in distress,

>   even anguish as severe as childbirth pains.

לְךָ תַּקְרִיב קֶרֶב לִבָּהּ כְּקָרְבָּן

וְצַלְעוֹתָיו עֲצֵי אֵשׁ מַעֲרַכְתָּהּ

לְךָ תִשְׁפֹּךְ דְּמָעֶיהָ כְּנֶסֶךְ

וְאַנְחָתָהּ מְקוֹם עֶשֶׁן קְטָרְתָּהּ

לְךָ תֵּקַד בְּלֵב עֲקֹד וְתִשְׁקֹד

בְּקוֹל שִׂיחָה עֲלֵי פִתְחָהּ וְדַלְתָּהּ

לְךָ תִקְרַב כְּמוֹ עֶבֶד לְמוּל רַב

וְכַשִּׁפְחָה תְּצַפֶּה אֶל גְּבִרְתָּהּ

לְךָ תֵכַף וְתִפְרֹשׂ כַּף לְמוּל סַף

וְתִתְהַפֵּךְ וְתִשְׁתַּפֵּךְ בְּגַעְגָתָהּ

לְךָ תֶהְמֶה וְלֹא תִדְמֶה וְתִדְמֶה

לְצִפּוֹר קוֹנְתָה לָנוּד בְּרִשְׁתָּהּ

לְךָ תָקוּם חֲצוֹת לַיְלָה וְתִשְׁמֹר

לְסַפֵּר מַלְאֲכוֹתֶיךָ מְלַאכְתָּהּ

לְךָ תִכְלֶה וּפָנֶיךָ תְחַלֶּה

בְּבֹר כַּפָּהּ וְנִקְיוֹן מַחֲשַׁבְתָּהּ

רְפָא שִׁבְרָהּ הֱיֵה שִׂבְרָהּ וְעֶזְרָהּ

קְרָא יִשְׁעָהּ מְחֵה פִשְׁעָהּ בְּגִשְׁתָּהּ

רְאֵה עָנְיָהּ שְׁמַע בִּכְיָהּ לְךָ יָהּ

בְּמָקוֹם בִּלְתְּךָ אֵין שָׁם וּבִלְתָּהּ

To You she brings her heart, a sacrifice,

　　her ribs like wood arranged upon an altar.

To You she pours libations of her tears;

　　her sighs are like the smoke of incense.

To You she bows, she binds her heart, abounds

　　in prayer at all her entrances and gates,

To You comes forth humbly as a slave,

　　humbly as a lady's maid toward her mistress.

To You she spreads her palms, toward Your threshold bows,

　　overwhelmed at reaching it.

To You she utters cries unceasing,

　　like a netted bird that longs to fly.

To You she rises in the night, keeps vigil,

　　makes her life's work to recount Your deeds.

To You her feelings surge. Before Your face

　　she makes her supplication

　　pure in mouth and thought.

Heal her injuries. Be her hope and help.

　　Summon her salvation, wipe away her fault

　　as she draws near.

See her sorrow, hear her weeping, God,

　　in a place where there is no one,

　　only You and she.

גְּמוּל תָּשִׁיב וְלָהּ תּוֹשִׁיב וְתַקְשִׁיב

לְשַׁוְעָתָהּ וְדִמְעָתָהּ בְּרִדְתָּהּ

לַעַג שַׁדַּי לְצָרִים לָעֲגוּ לָהּ

נָקֹם נִקְמַת כְּלִמָּתָהּ וּבָשְׁתָּהּ

הֱיֵה מֵצַר לְצוּר מִבְצָר בְּמֵצַר

וְאַל תַּסְגֵּר יְחִידָה שֶׁגְּדַלְתָּהּ

וְלֹא אוֹיֵב יְחָרְפָהּ וְתִשָּׂא

וְלֹא אַכְזָר יְצוּדֶהָ בְּלֶכְתָּהּ

אֲבָל אַנְשֵׁי שְׁלוֹמָהּ בָּגְדוּ בָהּ

וְדָמָה וַחֲמָסָהּ עַל חֲבֶרְתָּהּ

אֲנִי כָל־עֵת אֲבַקֵּשׁ אֶת־שְׁלוֹמָם

וְהֵמָּה בִקְשׁוּ נַפְשִׁי לְקַחְתָּהּ

וְאָמְנָם כִּי פְרִי הָעֵץ בְּשָׁרְשׁוֹ

וְהַמָּשָׁל אֱמֶת כָּאֵם כְּבִתָּהּ.

Requite her duly: Grant her rest,

>grant her a hearing as she pours her tears.

O God Almighty, mock the foes who mock her.

>Avenge her shame and her humiliation.

Be a fortress, be a Rock against her foes.

>Do not abandon her, the child You raised.

It is no enemy who taunts her—she could bear that—

>no stranger stalking her when she goes out,

but her intimates who have betrayed her.

>Her blood and outrage are on her companions' heads.

I am always working for their welfare:

>they keep trying to destroy my soul.

What else can one expect? The fruit is in the root.

>"Like the mother, so the daughter"—

>the maxim holds.

שְׂאִי עַיִן יְחִידָתִי לְצוּרֵךְ

וְזִכְרִי בּוֹרְאֵךְ בִּימֵי בְּחוּרֵךְ

לְפָנָיו צַעֲקִי לַיְל וְיוֹמָם

וְלִשְׁמוֹ זַמְּרִי תָמִיד בְּשִׁירֵךְ

מְנָת חֶלְקֵךְ וְכוֹסֵךְ בָּאֲדָמָה

וּמִבְטָחֵךְ בְּצֵאתֵךְ מִבְּשָׂרֵךְ

הֲלֹא הֵכִין לְפָנָיו לָךְ מְנוּחָה

וּמִתַּחַת לְכִסְאוֹ שָׁם דְּבִירֵךְ

אֲנִי עַל כֵּן אֲבָרֵךְ אֶת־אֲדֹנָי

כְּמוֹ כָל־הַנְּשָׁמָה לוֹ תְבָרֵךְ.

LIFT YOUR EYE to God, my precious soul.

    While you are young, give thought to Him Who made you.

Night and day, cry out to Him, and in your songs

    make constant mention of His Name.

He is your portion and your lot on earth,

    your only trust when once you leave this flesh.

Next to Him He has a resting place,

    a home prepared for you beneath His throne.

That is why I bless the Name of God,

    as every soul gives blessings to His Name.

שְׁאֵלוּנִי סְעִפַּי הַתְּמֵהִים
לְמִי תָרוּץ כְּגַלְגַּלֵּי גְבוֹהִים
לְאֵל חַיַּי תְּשׁוּקַת מַאֲוַיַּי
וְנַפְשִׁי עִם בְּשָׂרִי לוֹ כְמֵהִים
מְשׁוֹשִׂי עִם מְנָת כּוֹסִי בְּעוֹשִׂי
אֲשֶׁר עֵת אֶזְכְּרָה אוֹתוֹ וְאָהִים
הֲיִנְעַם שִׁיר לְנִשְׁמָתִי עֲדֵי כִי
תְבָרֵךְ שֵׁם אֲדֹנָי הָאֱלֹהִים.

MY MIND WAS asking me in wonderment,

> "Where are you speeding, swift as heaven's spheres?"

I say, "My lust is for the living God.

> To Him my soul and body yearn—

my joy, my lot in life, my Maker.

> It thrills me just to say His Name."

Can any song delight my soul unless

> it bless the Name of God, the Lord of lords?

שְׁחִי לָאֵל יְחִידָה הַחֲכָמָה
וְרוּצִי לַעֲבֹד אוֹתוֹ בְּאֵימָה
לְעוֹלָמֵךְ פְּנִי לֵילֵךְ וְיוֹמֵךְ
וְלָמָּה תִרְדְּפִי הֶבֶל וְלָמָּה

מְשׁוּלָה אַתְּ בְּחַיּוּתֵךְ לְאֵל חַי
אֲשֶׁר נֶעְלָם כְּמוֹ אַתְּ נֶעֱלָמָה
הֲלֹא אִם יוֹצְרֵךְ טָהוֹר וְנָקִי
דְּעִי כִּי כֵן טְהוֹרָה אַתְּ וְתַמָּה
חָסִין יִשָּׂא שְׁחָקִים עַל זְרוֹעוֹ
כְּמוֹ תִשְׂאִי גְוִיָּה נֶאֱלָמָה

זְמִירוֹת קַדְּמִי נַפְשִׁי לְצוּרֵךְ
אֲשֶׁר לֹא שָׂם דְּמוּתֵךְ בָּאֲדָמָה
קְרָבַי בָּרְכוּ תָּמִיד לְצוּרְכֶם
אֲשֶׁר לִשְׁמוֹ תְּהַלֵּל כָּל־נְשָׁמָה.

SUBMIT TO GOD, my cerebrating soul,
    and run to worship Him in holy dread.
Devote your nights and days to your true world.
    Why, why so bent on chasing empty breath?

For you, like God, have everlasting life,
    and He, like you, is hidden from the eye.
And if your Maker is immaculate and pure,
    you too are pure, you too are innocent.
The Mighty One bears heaven on His arm,
    just as you bear the mute and mortal clay.

My soul, greet God, your Rock, with gifts of praise,
    for nothing has He put on earth like you.
My body, bless your Rock forevermore,
    to Whom the soul of All sings ever praise.

שַׁחַר אֲבַקֶּשְׁךָ צוּרִי וּמִשְׂגַּבִּי

אֶעֱרֹךְ לְפָנֶיךָ שַׁחְרִי וְגַם עַרְבִּי

לִפְנֵי גְדֻלָּתְךָ אֶעֱמֹד וְאֶבָּהֵל

כִּי עֵינְךָ תִרְאֶה כָל־מַחְשְׁבוֹת לִבִּי

מַה־זֶּה אֲשֶׁר יוּכַל הַלֵּב וְהַלָּשׁוֹן

לַעֲשׂוֹת וּמַה־כֹּחַ רוּחִי בְּתוֹךְ קִרְבִּי

הִנֵּה לְךָ תִיטַב זִמְרַת אֱנוֹשׁ עַל כֵּן

אוֹדְךָ בְּעוֹד תִּהְיֶה נִשְׁמַת אֱלוֹהַּ בִּי

AT DAWN I COME to You, my Rock, my Strength;

    I offer You my dawn and evening prayers.

Before Your majesty I stand in fear,

    because Your eye observes my secret thoughts.

What is there that man's mind and mouth

    can make? What power is there in my body's breath?

And yet the songs of man delight You. Therefore I

    shall praise You while God's breath remains in me.

שִׁחַרְתִּיךָ בְּכָל־שַׁחְרִי וְנִשְׁפִּי
וּפָרַשְׂתִּי לְךָ כַּפַּי וְאַפִּי
לְךָ אֶהֱמֶה בְּלֵב צָמֵא וְאֶדְמֶה
לְדַל שׁוֹאֵל עֲלֵי פִתְחִי וְסִפִּי

מְרוֹמוֹת לֹא יְכִילוּךָ לְשִׁבְתָּךְ
וְאוּלָם יֵשׁ מְקוֹמְךָ תוֹךְ סְעִפִּי
הֲלֹא אֶצְפֹּן בְּלִבִּי שֵׁם כְּבוֹדְךָ
וְגָבַר חִשְׁקְךָ עַד יַעֲבָר־פִּי

אֲנִי עַל כֵּן אֲהוֹדֶה שֵׁם אֲדֹנָי
בְּעוֹד נִשְׁמַת אֱלֹהִים חַי בְּאַפִּי

AT MORNING and at evening I seek You.
  I offer You my face and outspread palms.
For You I yearn, to You I turn, Your grace to earn,
  like someone at my door who asks for alms.

The heavens do not have room for You to dwell,
  and yet You have a palace in my mind.
For in my heart, I hide Your Holy Name;
  Your love spills over, cannot be confined.

And so I praise God with my poetry,
  while yet He breathes the living soul in me.

שְׁלֹשָׁה נוֹסְדוּ יַחַד לְעֵינַי

יְשִׂימוּן זִכְרְךָ תָּמִיד לְפָנַי

לְשָׁמֶיךָ אֲנִי אַזְכִּיר שְׁמֶךָ

וְהֵם עָדַי לְעֵדַי נֶאֱמָנַי

מָקוֹם שִׁבְתִּי יְעוֹרֵר מַחֲשַׁבְתִּי

בְּרַקְעוֹ אֶזְכְּרָה רֹקַע אֲדָנַי

הֲגִיג לִבִּי בְּהַבִּיטִי בְּקִרְבִּי

בְּכָל־עֵת בָּרְכִי נַפְשִׁי אֲדֹנָי.

THREE THINGS there are, together in my eye

    that keep the thought of You forever nigh.

I think about Your Great and Holy Name

    whenever I look up and see the sky.

My thoughts are roused to know how I was made,

    seeing the earth's expanse, where I abide.

The musings of my mind, when I look inside—

    At all times, "O my soul, bless Adonai."

שְׁפַל רוּחַ שְׁפַל בֶּרֶךְ וְקוֹמָה

אֲקַדֶּמְךָ בְּרֹב פַּחַד וְאֵימָה

לְפָנֶיךָ אֲנִי נֶחְשָׁב בְּעֵינִי

כְּתוֹלַעַת קְטַנָּה בָּאֲדָמָה

מְלוֹא עוֹלָם אֲשֶׁר אֵין קֵץ לְגָדְלוֹ

הֲכָמוֹנִי יְהַלֶּלְךָ וּבַמָּה

הֲדָרְךָ לֹא יְכִילוּן מַלְאֲכֵי רוֹם

וְעַל אַחַת אֲנִי כַּמָּה וְכַמָּה

הֵטִיבוֹתָ וְהִגְדַּלְתָּ חֲסָדִים

וְלָךְ תַּגְדִּיל לְהוֹדוֹת הַנְּשָׁמָה.

WITH LOWLY SPIRIT, lowered knee and head,

    in fear I come; I offer You my dread.

But facing You, I know I've no more worth

    than any little worm that crawls the earth.

O fullness of the world, Infinity—

    What praise can come, if any can, from me?

Your splendor is not contained by the hosts on high,

    and how much less capacity have I!

Infinite You, and infinite Your ways.

    Therefore the soul expands to sing Your praise.

שְׂשׂוֹנִי רַב בְּךָ שׁוֹכֵן מְעוֹנִי

זְכַרְתִּיךָ וְנָס מֶנִּי יְגוֹנִי

לְךָ חֶסֶד וְיֵשׁ עָלַי לְהוֹדוֹת

וְאֵין בַּמֶּה לְבַד הֶגְיוֹן לְשׁוֹנִי

מְרוֹמִים לֹא יְכִילוּן תַּעֲצוּמָךְ

וְאֵיךְ יוּכַל שְׂאֵתוֹ רַעְיוֹנִי

הֲבִינֵנִי וְחָנֵּנִי נְכוֹחָה

וְיָפֵק אֶת־רְצוֹנֶךָ רְצוֹנִי

קְחָה שֶׁבַח מְקוֹם זֶבַח וְיִיטַב

כְּקָרְבָּנִי וּמִנְחַת זִכְרוֹנִי

טְהָר־עַיִן פְּקַח עַיִן לְעָנְיִי

שְׁלַח אוֹרְךָ וְהָאֵר עִוְרוֹנִי

נְצֹר גֹּדֶל חֲסָדֶיךָ לְמַעְנִי

יְהִי סֵתֶר עֲלֵי גֹדֶל עֲוֹנִי

כְּמוֹ שִׁמְךָ לְפִקָּדוֹן בְּלִבִּי

תְּהִי רוּחִי בְּיָדְךָ פִקְּדוֹנִי.

MY JOY IN YOU is great, O You Who dwells on high.

    I think of You and all my sorrow vanishes.

All grace is Yours. For it, I owe You thanks,

      but all I have to thank You with

      is what is on my tongue.

The heavens cannot contain the vastness of Your self,

      so how am I to hold it in my mind?

Grant me wisdom, grant me to do right,

      grant that my will may fulfill Your own.

Accept my praise as if it were a sacrifice,

      as dear as offerings to You would be.

Clear-sighted God, behold my misery,

      and send Your light, that I, though blind, may see.

Maintain Your kindness always, for my sake,

      and may it keep me from my grievous sins.

Just as Your Name is held in trust inside my heart,

      so may You hold my soul in trust within Your hand.

שַׁעַר אֲשֶׁר נִסְגַּר
קוּמָה פְּתָחֵהוּ
וּצְבִי אֲשֶׁר בָּרַח
אֵלַי שְׁלָחֵהוּ

לְיוֹם בּוֹאֲךָ עָדַי
לָלִין בְּבֵין שָׁדַי
שָׁם רֵיחֲךָ הַטּוֹב
עָלַי תְּנִיחֵהוּ

מַה־זֶּה דְמוּת דּוֹדֵךְ
כַּלָּה יְפֵה פִיָּה
כִּי תֹאמְרִי אֵלַי
שְׁלָחָה וְקָחֵהוּ
הַהוּא יְפֵה עַיִן
אָדֹם וְטוֹב רֹאִי

רֵעִי וְדוֹדִי זֶה
קוּמָה מְשָׁחֵהוּ.

"THE GATE long shut—

        get up and throw it wide;

    the stag long fled—

        send him to my side.

When one day you come

        to lie between my breasts,

    that day your scent

        will cling to me like wine."

"How shall I know his face, O lovely bride,

        the lover you are asking me to send?

    A ruddy face with lovely eyes,

        a handsome man to see?"

"Yes, that's my love! Yes, that's my friend!

    Anoint that one for me!"

שַׁחַר עָלָה אֵלִי
דּוֹדִי וְלֵךְ עִמִּי
כִּי צָמְאָה נַפְשִׁי
לִרְאוֹת בְּנֵי עַמִּי

לְךָ אֶפְרְשָׂה מִטּוֹת
זָהָב בְּאוּלַמִּי
אֶעֱרָךְ־לְךָ שֻׁלְחָן
אֶעֱרָךְ־לְךָ לַחְמִי

מִזְרָק אֲמַלֵּא לָךְ
מֵאֶשְׁכְּלוֹת כַּרְמִי
וּשְׁתֵה בְּטוּב לֵבָב
יִיטַב לְךָ טַעְמִי

הִנֵּה בְּךָ אֶשְׂמַח
שִׂמְחַת נְגִיד עַמִּי
בֶּן־עַבְדְּךָ יִשַׁי
הָרֹאשׁ לְבֵית לַחְמִי.

COME TO ME at dawn, love,
      carry me away;
For in my heart I have a thirst
      to see my folk today.

For you, love, golden mats
      within my halls I'll spread.
I'll set my table for you,
      I'll serve you my own bread.

A drink from my own vineyards
      I'll pour to fill your cup—
heartily you'll drink, love,
      heartily you'll sup.

I'll take my pleasure with you
      as once I had such joy
with Jesse's son, my people's prince,
      that Bethlehem boy.

שׁוֹכֵב עֲלֵי מִטּוֹת זָהָב בְּאַרְמוֹנִי
מָתַי יְצוּעֲי יָהּ תָּכִין לְאַדְמוֹנִי
לָמָּה צְבִי נֶחְמָד תִּישַׁן וְהַשַּׁחַר
עָלָה כְנֵס עַל רֹאשׁ שְׂנִירִי וְחֶרְמוֹנִי
מֵעַל פְּרָאִים סוּר וּנְטֵה לְיַעֲלַת חֵן
הִנְנִי לְכָמוֹךְ וְאַתְּ טוֹב לְכָמוֹנִי
הַבָּא בְּאַרְמוֹנִי יִמְצָא בְמַטְמוֹנִי
עָסִיס וְרִמּוֹנִי מוֹרִי וְקִנָּמוֹנִי.

O YOU ASLEEP on golden couches in my palace spread—
When, O Lord, will You prepare my red-cheeked
champion's bed?
Why asleep, my handsome stag? Why asleep, my dear,
when dawn has risen like a flag on Hermon and Senir?
Turn away from desert-asses, turn to the gazelle;
I am right for one like you, and your kind suits me well.
He who comes to visit me, my precious stores will find:
my myrrh, my pomegranates, my cinnamon, my wine.

שׁוֹכַנְתְּ בַּשָּׂדֶה עִם אָהֳלֵי כוּשָׁן
עִמְדִי לְרֹאשׁ כַּרְמֶל צְפִי לְהַר בָּשָׁן
לַגַּן אֲשֶׁר נֶחְמַס כַּלָּה שְׂאִי עֵינֵךְ
וּרְאִי עֲרוּגָתֵךְ כִּי נִמְלְאָה שׁוֹשָׁן

מַה־לָּךְ יְפֵה עַיִן כִּי תַעֲזֹב גַּנִּי
לִרְעוֹת בְּגַן יָקְשָׁן תַּחַת עֲצֵי דִישָׁן
הָבָה רְדָה לַגַּן תֹּאכַל מְגָדִים שָׁם
וּבְחֵיק יְפַת עַיִן תִּשְׁכַּב וְגַם תִּישָׁן.

"O MAIDEN who resides in Kushan's distant desert tents—
    Go and look toward Mount Carmel, gaze at
        Mount Bashan.
Raise your eyes, my bride, toward the ruined garden,
    and see how blooming lilies fill your garden beds."

"Why did you ever leave my garden, O my handsome love,
    to care for Yokshan's flocks underneath Dishan's trees?
Come join me in that garden, there eat your fill of fruit,
    there take your rest against the breast of the girl with
        lovely eyes."

שַׁעַר פְּתַח דּוֹדִי

קוּמָה פְּתַח שַׁעַר

כִּי נִבְהֲלָה נַפְשִׁי

גַּם נִשְׂעֲרָה שַׂעַר

לִי לָעֲגָה שִׁפְחַת

אִמִּי וְרָם לִבִּי

יַעַן שָׁמֹעַ אֶל

קוֹל צַעֲקַת נַעַר

מִנִּי חֲצוֹת לַיְלָה

פֶּרֶא רְדָפַנִי

אַחֲרֵי אֲשֶׁר רָמַס

אוֹתִי חֲזִיר יַעַר

הַקֵּץ אֲשֶׁר נֶחְתַּם

הוֹסִיף עֲלֵי מַכְאוֹב

לִבִּי וְאֵין מֵבִין

לִי וַאֲנִי בַעַר.

OPEN WIDE the gate, my love,

    open wide the gate.

For terror's in my heart, my love,

    the storm does not abate.

My mother's maid is mocking me,

    her heart is great with pride,

because the Lord once listened

    to her little one when he cried.

Since midnight I'm chased from place to place,

    by the desert-ass;

trampled before by the forest-boar,

    everywhere harassed.

Keeping the end concealed, love,

    only makes worse the pain.

In ignorance I suffer, love,

    with no one to explain.

שָׁלוֹם לָךְ דּוֹדִי

הַצַּח וְהָאַדְמוֹן
שָׁלוֹם לָךְ מֵאֵת
רַקָּה כְּמוֹ רִמּוֹן
לִקְרַאת אֲחוֹתָךְ רוּץ
צֵא נָא לְהוֹשִׁיעָה
וּצְלַח כְּבֶן־יִשַׁי
רַבַּת בְּנֵי עַמּוֹן

מַה־לָּךְ יְפֵה פִיָּה
כִּי תְעוֹרְרִי אַהֲבָה
וּתְצַלְצְלִי קוֹלֵךְ
כִּמְעִיל בְּקוֹל פַּעֲמוֹן
הָעֵת אֲשֶׁר תַּחְפָּץ
אַהֲבָה אָחִישֶׁנָּה
עַתָּה וְעָלַיִךְ
אֵרֵד כְּטַל חֶרְמוֹן.

SHE:

"GREETINGS TO YOU, red-cheeked friend,

    greetings to you from the girl

    with the pomegranate brow.

Run to meet her—your beloved—

    hurry out to rescue her!

Charge, like David, valiant king

    when he took Rabbah, the city."

HE:

"Why, my beauty, why just now

    do you choose to rouse my love,

set your lovely voice to ringing

    like a priest's robe hung with bells?

When the time for loving comes,

    then you'll see me hurrying.

Then I will come down to you

    as on Mount Hermon drips the dew."

327

שְׁלֹף חַרְבְּךָ דּוֹדִי הַצַּח וְהָאָדֹם
וְשִׁית אוֹיְבַי תַּחַת כַּף רַגְלְךָ לַהֲדֹם
לַיִל כְּבָר פָּנָה הַיּוֹם כְּבָר חָנָה
קוּמָה צְלַח וּרְכַב קוּמָה וְאַל תֵּרָדֹם

מֵאָז אֲנִי יוֹצֵא אָחוֹת לְהוֹשִׁיעֵךְ
גַּם עִם יְרִיבַיִךְ אָרִיב וְלֹא אָדֹם

הִנֵּה מְעַט חֵילֵי שָׂרֵי צְבָא עַמָּךְ
כִּי נֻגְּפוּ אוֹתוֹ מַלְכֵי עֲרָב וֶאֱדֹם

הִנֵּה אֲנִי אָקוּם אֶרְכַּב עֲלֵי סוּסִי
אֶרֶץ יְרִיבַיִךְ אֶהְפֹּךְ אֲזַי כִּסְדֹם.

"**DRAW YOUR** sword, my shining, red-cheeked love,
and make my enemies a cushion for your feet.
Night is over, day is here at last.
Get up, mount, and ride! Get up! Enough of sleep!"

"The day I sally forth, my dear, to rescue you,
you'll see me making war unflagging on your foes."

"Your people's troops, their officers, are far too few,
depleted by the troops of Christians and Arabians."

"But I am ready. Once I mount my stallion,
I'll turn their land into a ruin like Sodóm."

שְׁכָחִי יְגוֹנֵךְ

נֶפֶשׁ הוֹמִיָּה	לָמָּה תִּפְחֲדִי
מִמְּצוּקֵי נְשִׁיָּה	מָחָר גּוּפֵךְ
יִשְׁכֹּן תַּחְתִּיָּה	הַכֹּל נִשְׁכָּח
כְּאִלּוּ לֹא הָיָה	

נֶפֶשׁ הַשְׂכִּילִי

וּמִמָּוֶת חִגְלִי

וְלָאֵל הוֹחִילִי

אוּלַי תּוֹעִילִי

וְנַפְשֵׁךְ תַּצִּילִי

בְּשׁוּבֵךְ אֶל קוֹנֵךְ

יוֹם תִּצְפִּי פְּעֻלַּת קִנְיָנֵךְ

נֶפֶשׁ נִדְהָמָה	לָמָּה וְלָמָּה
עֲלֵי תֵבֵל אֲדָמָה	תִּלְבְּשִׁי שְׁמָמָה
גְּוִיָּה נֶאֱלָמָה	כְּצֵאת הַנְּשָׁמָה

בְּשׁוּבֵךְ אֶל יְסוֹדֵךְ

לֹא תִשְׂאִי בְּיָדֵךְ

מְאוּמָה מִכְּבוֹדֵךְ

יוֹם יָחִישׁ נוֹדֵךְ

כְּצִפּוֹר אֶל קִנֵּךְ

יוֹם תִּצְפִּי פְּעֻלַּת קִנְיָנֵךְ

STOP YOUR sorrowing,   suffering soul.
Why should you fear   the world's woes?
Tomorrow your body   will dwell underground,
all lost to mind   as if it never were.

       Be wise, my soul:

       Fear death,

       trust God.

       Maybe you'll manage

       to save yourself

    when you return to your Maker

    the day your deeds are requited.

Why, why,   O agonized soul,
give such care   to the world of decay?
When the soul flies away,   when the body is still,

       once back at your source,

       you'll have in your hands

       no honors or wealth—

       on the day when you speed

    like a bird to his nest,

    on the day your deeds are requited.

מַה־לָּךְ נְסוּכָה   בְּדֶרֶךְ לֹא מְשׂוּכָה

אֲשֶׁר בָּהּ מְלוּכָה   תֵּהָפֵךְ מְבוּכָה

תִּדְמֶה אֲרוּכָה   וְהִיא קֶשֶׁת דְּרוּכָה

כָּל־יְקָרָהּ כָּזָב

וְכָל־טוּבָהּ אַכְזָב

וְהוּא נָמֵס וְזָב

וְלַאֲחֵרִים נֶעֱזָב

וּמַה־יּוֹעִיל הוֹנֵךְ

יוֹם תְּצַפִּי פְּעֻלַּת קִנְיָנֵךְ

הַחַי גֶּפֶן   וְהַמָּוֶת בּוֹצֵר

וּבַאֲשֶׁר יֵלֵךְ   צְעָדָיו הוּא נוֹצֵר

שׁוּבִי נַפְשִׁי   לְבַקֵּשׁ הַיּוֹצֵר

הַיּוֹם קָצֵר   וְרָחוֹק הֶחָצֵר

נֶפֶשׁ שׁוֹבֵבָה

דַּי לָךְ בְּפַת חֲרֵבָה

וְשִׁכְבִי מַעֲצֵבָה

וְזִכְרִי מַצֵּבָה

וְגוּרִי יוֹם דִּינֵךְ

יוֹם תְּצַפִּי פְּעֻלַּת קִנְיָנֵךְ

What are you doing, O soul,   on this road not long,

this place where dominion   is merely damnation?

It seems so soothing   but really is death.

     Its riches are false,

     its wealth a mirage

     that melts into sewage,

     and ends up with others.

     What good is your wealth

     on the day your deeds are requited?

Living men are a vine;   death picks the grapes.

Wherever men go,   he watches their steps.

Back, my soul, back!   Seek your Creator.

The time is so short,   so distant the goal!

     O wayward soul:

     all you need is a crust.

     Lie down lamenting,

     brood on your tomb,

     and fear God's judgment

     on the day your sins are requited.

חָרְדִי כְּיוֹנָה   עֲנִיָּה אֶבְיוֹנָה

זִכְרִי בְּכָל־עֵת   מְנוּחָה עֶלְיוֹנָה

קָרְאִי מְעוֹנָה   בְּכָל־רֶגַע וְעוֹנָה

בְּכִי תָּמִיד לְעֵינָיו

וְהִתְחַנְּנִי לְפָנָיו

וְהָפִיקִי רְצוֹנָיו

וְאָז מַלְאֲכֵי מְעוֹנָיו

יְבִיאוּךְ אֶל גַּנֶּךְ

יוֹם תְּצַפִּי פְּעֻלַּת קִנְיָנֶךְ

334

Like a dove, shudder,   poor, wretched soul.

Always be mindful   of that rest supernal.

Cry out to heaven   each moment, each season.

Weep to Him always.

Petition Him ever.

Above all: Do His will.

Then His high angels

will lead you to paradise

on the day your deeds are requited.

שָׁפְכִי לְצוּר לִבֵּךְ
נַפְשֵׁךְ וְגַם קִרְבֵּךְ
הוֹדִי לְמִשְׂגַּבֵּךְ
שַׁחֲרֵךְ וְגַם עַרְבֵּךְ

לְנֶגְדֵּךְ וְלִסְבִיבֵךְ
קוּמֵךְ וּמִשְׁכָּבֵךְ
יַעַל בְּמַחְשָׁבֵךְ
בְּלֶכְתֵּךְ וּמוֹשָׁבֵךְ

מַעֲלָל בְּהֵיטִיבֵךְ
יִרְצֵךְ וְיַקְשִׁיבֵךְ
יִפֶן לְמַעְצָבֵךְ
יַבִּיט לְמַכְאוֹבֵךְ

הִנֵּה גְמוּל טוּבֵךְ
יְשַׁלֵּם בְּיוֹם שׁוּבֵךְ
אֵלָיו וְיוֹשִׁיבֵךְ
אֶצְלוֹ וְיַקְרִיבֵךְ.

POUR OUT your heart to God—
     your body and your soul.
Praise Him, Who is your refuge,
     morning and evening.

In front of you, around you,
     when you stand or lie,
when you walk or sit,
     have Him in your thoughts.

Make your actions good ones—
     He'll favor you and hear you,
turn and see your sorrow,
     be attentive to your pain.

He will repay you for the good
     you've done when you return
to Him. Then He will bring you near,
     and seat you by His side.

הָאֵימָה תִּתְכַּבֵּד

הַבִּירָה תֶּעֱשַׁן

הַגְּבוּרָה תִּתְגַּבֵּר

הַדְּמָמָה תֶּהֱמֶה

הַהוֹגִים יִצְרָחוּ

הַוְּעוּדִים יִצָּוְחוּ

הַזֹּהַר יִנָּטֶה

הַחִצִּים יְרוֹצְצוּ

הַטִּיסָה תִּתְעוֹפֵף

הַיִּרְאָה תִנָּתֵן

הַכִּסֵּא יִתְרוֹמֵם

הַלַּהַב יְשׁוֹטֵט

הַמֶּרְכָּבָה תָּנוּעַ

הַנִּצָּבִים יִרְעָדוּ

הַשְּׂרָפִים יִסְעָרוּ

הָעוֹמְדִים יְרוֹפְפוּן

הַפַּחַד יִפֹּל

הַצְּבָאוֹת יִצְהָלוּ

הַקּוֹל יִשָּׁמַע

הָרַעַם יִגְעֶה

THE TERROR takes on glory.

The Temple smokes.

The Power prevails.

The Silence surges.

The Worshipers shout.

The Assembled cry out.

The Splendor spreads.

The Lightning darts.

The Angel-Flight flutters.

The Awe is imparted.

The Throne ascends.

The Flame roams.

The Chariot rolls.

The Attendants quake.

The Seraphs storm.

The Presences fail.

The Fear falls.

The Throngers thrill.

The Clangor sounds.

The Thunder roars.

הַשֵּׁם יִזָּכֵר

תּוֹךְ פִּי קְדוֹשֵׁי מַעְלָה

הַיּוֹדְעִים כֹּחוֹ

הַמַּכִּירִים חֵילוֹ

הַשּׁוֹמְעִים בַּת קוֹלוֹ

הָרָצִים לְהַלְלוֹ

יִקְרְאוּ זֶה אֶל זֶה

וְיֹאמְרוּ זֶה לָזֶה

וְיַעֲנוּ זֶה אֶת־זֶה

וִיקַבְּלוּ זֶה מִזֶּה

גּוֹשׁוּ עוּשׁוּ חוּשׁוּ וְנַעֲרִיץ לְמֶלֶךְ הַכָּבוֹד זֶה.

The Name is uttered

by the mouths of the high holy ones

who know His might,

    who are aware of His troops,

        who hear His voice,

            who run to praise Him,

who call to one another,

    say to one another,

        respond to one another,

            accept from one another:

"Come! Hasten! Hurry! Let us praise this King of Glory!"

שֶׁמֶשׁ כְּחָתָן יַעֲטֶה סוּת אוֹר

מֵהוֹדְךָ נֶאֱצַל וְלֹא נֶעְדָּר

לָמַד לְסוֹבֵב אֶל פְּאַת מַעֲרָב

מִשְׁתַּחֲוֶה אֶל כִּסְאֲךָ נֶאְדָּר

מִיוֹם עֲבָדְךָ שָׁר וְכֵן עָבֵד

יְהַדֵּר פְּנֵי רַבּוֹ יְהִי נֶהְדָּר

הוּא יוֹם בְּיוֹם מִשְׁתַּחֲוֶה לְךָ גַּם

אַתְּ מַעֲטֶה עָלָיו מְעִיל הָדָר.

THE SUN PUTS on a bridegroom's suit of light,

    a never-failing light that shines from You.

Each evening he turns to face the west,

    and bows toward Your throne, O Mighty One.

Serving You has made him powerful,

    as courtiers gain honor honoring their lords.

Each day, he bows before You when he sets,

    and You in turn enwrap him

    in a robe of splendor.

NOTES

Pp. 10–11

Aram once lamented Beor's son: Probably refers to Balaam the son of Beor, the Aramean wizard hired by Balak the son of Zippor to curse the Israelites as they encamped in Moab (Numbers 22–24). The figure of Balaam, a non-Jew thought to be endowed with knowledge of the divine world, is uncannily apt for the situation that Ibn Gabirol describes here. But there is no tradition of his being lamented by the Arameans or anyone else.

Pp. 14–15

Azázel: A desert demon mentioned in Lev. 16:8.

Pp. 16–17

reserved: An allusion to the ancient legend that God put away the light created on the first day of Creation (Gen. 1:3–4) and stored it for the World to Come, replacing it for the present with the ordinary light of the sun, moon, and stars. Ibn Gabirol identifies the hidden light with the intellect.

Yekutiel: Besides being the name of Ibn Gabirol's patron (see above, p. xi), Yekutiel is one of the seven names of Moses in rabbinic tradition.

Pp. 20–21

Pharaoh's viceroy: Joseph, who, according to Genesis 37, was seventeen when sold to an Egyptian courtier and rose to become Pharaoh's second in command.

Pp. 24–25

On ben Pelet: A participant in the rebellion of Koraḥ against the leadership of Moses and Aaron in the wilderness (Numbers 16–17). It is hard to see why Ibn Gabirol singled out On, who played no notable part in the rebellion.

a jewel . . . a coal: An allusion to the legend that when the infant Moses was confronted by Pharaoh with jewels and coals, he put a coal in his mouth;

this story is supposed to explain the speech impediment to which Moses refers in Exod. 4:10. Ibn Gabirol's verse also alludes to Isaiah's summons to prophecy (Isa. 6:5–7) and to God's turning Balaam's curse into a blessing (Numbers 22–24).

Sodom's men: An allusion to the story in Gen. 19:1–11.

Pp. 36–37

The third verse from the end of this poem has been omitted from the translation as being a mere doublet of the following verse.

Pp. 44–45

a diadem for kings: Sixteen verses of panegyric for the unnamed patron have been omitted.

Pp. 54–55

geonim: The heads of the academies of talmudic scholarship, especially of the academies of Sura and Pumbedita, then located in Baghdad.

Pp. 64–65

Sabea and Dedan: Nations mentioned in the Bible, here used merely to signify distant lands.

Pp. 72–73

elevate your wisdom's standard: An echo of Moses' healing action in Num. 21:9.

Pp. 74–75

her high abodes: The referent of the pronoun is not specified; it seems to be an allegorical female figure representing divine wisdom.

Pp. 78–79

she, the Holy Ark . . .: Israel and the dignitaries lamented in the poem are compared to various sacred paraphernalia described in Exodus 25 and 28.

Pp. 84–85

Day of Gathering: I.e., death.

Pp. 106–7

al-Andalus: The Arabic name of the Iberian Peninsula.

Land of Beauty: I.e., the Land of Israel (Dan. 11:16).

Pp. 108–9

Ben-Levi: This person has not been identified; the reading is uncertain.

Pp. 110–11

Ah! What has become of me: From these words to the end, the poem is in Arabic.

Pp. 116–17

Ashkelon babble: Ashkelon was a Philistine city in biblical times, its language presumably unintelligible to Jews.

Pp. 118–19

Mondays, Thursdays, and Mondays: When disaster called for a public fast, it was usually held on Monday, Thursday, and the following Monday.

Pp. 120–21

Solomon: The poet is not claiming that Solomon was literally his ancestor but is referring to the fact that Solomon was regarded as the archetypal master of wisdom and to the fact that Solomon was the poet's given name.

Pp. 122–23

Jeroboam: The story is recorded in 1 Kings 11:40.

Red Sea . . . Egyptians: The Egyptians, according to the biblical story, drowned in the Red Sea (Exod. 14:26–28).

Pp. 126–27

Asael: A swift runner named in 2 Sam. 2:18.

Jebusites: A people described as lame in 2 Sam. 5:8.

Pp. 128–29

Moses flung soot: Moses triggered the plague of boils by hurling handfuls of soot toward the sky (Exod. 9:8–12).

Pp. 130–31

Oholiav, Bezalel: Craftsmen charged with building the Tabernacle that was carried by the Israelites in the desert (Exod. 31:1–6).

River Beast . . . Jordan's rushing waters: The image of the hippopotamus allowing a river to rush into his open mouth comes from Job 40:23.

turned to blood: The plague of blood is described in Exod. 7:14–25.

Pp. 132–33

Ishmael . . . Gedaliah: The former was head of a conspiracy that killed the latter, the governor of Judaea, in 586 BCE. It is unclear why Ibn Gabirol chose these names for his two pustules.

Pp. 140–41

Minḥah, Kaddish: Minḥah is the afternoon service, recited between mid-afternoon and nightfall. It is considered meritorious to recite this and the other obligatory prayers as part of a congregation praying together in a synagogue; Kaddish is a prayer that may be recited only in the presence of a congregation.

Pp. 144–45

Seled: An obscure individual said in 1 Chron. 2:30 to have died childless.

Pp. 156–57

Samuel, now arisen: Samuel the Nagid (see introduction, p. xiii).

Ramah and Mizpah: Places associated with Samuel the Prophet (1 Sam. 7:16–17).

Pp. 164–65

Levites . . . sons of Levi: Samuel the Nagid, the dedicatee of this panegyric, often boasted of his descent from the tribe of Levi, which provided the ancient Temple with liturgical singers.

Ziba . . . Mephibosheth: The betrayal of the former by the latter is related in 2 Sam. 16:1–4 and 19:25–31.

sons of Amram: I.e., Moses and Aaron.

Heman, Asaph: Levites named in the Bible as Temple singers.

Hebron, Uziel, Mishael: More Temple singers named in the Bible.

Babylon, Iraq, Shinar: The Jews continued to call Iraq *Bavel* (denoting both the city Babylon and the territory of Babylonia) in Hebrew long after the Muslim conquests. Shinar is another Hebrew name for the region. The Jewish academies of Iraq, headed by sages known as geonim, were considered the leading centers of rabbinic learning until the mid-eleventh century.

father of all sages: Solomon. There is no verse in the books traditionally attributed to him (Proverbs, Ecclesiastes, Song of Songs) that is exactly like the admonition here, but several passages in the book of Proverbs, such as 25:8, make the same point.

Dunash, Menahem, Abun: All poets of the tenth century; the first two were part of the literary circle around the Cordoban Jewish courtier Ḥasdai Ibn Shaprut (c. 915–c. 970). Dunash was the first Hebrew poet to employ Arabic prosody in Hebrew, one of the hallmarks of the Hebrew Golden Age. Menaḥem, his contemporary and rival, rejected Dunash's innovations but is also regarded as one of the founders of the school. Abun is mentioned by several medieval authors, but none of his poems has survived.

bore his ear: In biblical law (Exod. 21:5–6), this action, done at the slave's request, turns a temporary slave into a permanent one.

"O God of Power! Raging God!" The opening line of one of Samuel the Nagid's greatest war poems, written in 1038. My translation, along with extensive introductory remarks, may be found in Joseph V. Montville, *Prelude to History: Muslims and Jews in the Medieval Mediterranean* (Lanham, Md.: Lexington,

2011), pp. 55–70; an abridged version appears in Olivia R. Constable, *Medieval Iberia* (Philadelphia: University of Pennsylvania Press, 1997), pp. 357–63; 2d ed. (2011), pp. 107–16.

Pp. 208–9

break through boundary-fences: This is Hebrew's proverbial way of expressing the idea of encroachment, derived from Deut. 19:14.

Pp. 214–15

The final verses of this poem, in which the poet responds to an unspecified attack, have been omitted.

Pp. 228–33

These poems are riddles on apples.

Pp. 238–39

laws of consanguinity: Lit., "like a student in tractate Yevamot." This is a notoriously difficult tractate of the Talmud, dealing, among other things, with the confusing subject of forbidden degrees of marriage.

Pp. 240–41

Ahasuerus's harem: Described in the book of Esther.

Pp. 248–49

The second part of this poem, consisting of panegyric, has been omitted.

Pp. 254–55

while lightning danced: In this and the following lines, the lightning in the cloud is the flashing wine inside its crystal cup.

Samuel the Nagid: This is the gratuitous slap referred to in the introduction (p. xxii). The poem on pp. 162–73 may be Ibn Gabirol's apology.

Pp. 268–69

Abigail, Jezebel: The former was a woman who thwarted her husband in order to support King David in his rebellion against King Saul, and later became one of David's wives (1 Samuel 25). The latter was the queen of King Ahab, who induced him to introduce Tyrian idolatry into the northern Israelite kingdom, arousing the implacable wrath of the prophet Elijah (1 Kings 18, 19; 2 Kings 9).

Pp. 272–73

Amnon, Tamar: A son and a daughter of David by different mothers. Amnon feigned illness in order to induce Tamar to visit him, and then raped her (2 Samuel 13). Ibn Gabirol's lighthearted use of this ugly story is astonishing.

Pp. 284–85

trusting the interpreter: There is a rabbinic tradition that the predictive power of a dream depends on the interpretation attached to it rather than on the dream itself.

Pp. 290–93

Ambiguous: Is the poem about the redemption of the Jewish people from exile, or about the redemption of the soul from the realm of matter?

Pp. 298–99

companions: The body, with its limbs and senses.

Pp. 310–11

"O my soul, bless Adonai": A verbatim quotation of Ps. 104:1.

Pp. 316–29

The poems in this group, for all their erotic imagery, are actually about the Jewish aspiration for the coming of a Messiah to bring about the end of the exiled state and the reestablishment of Jewish sovereignty in the Land of Israel. 351 Israel is depicted as a girl awaiting her lover, who is described in terms that sometimes relate to King David, believed to be the ancestor of the Messiah, and sometimes to God, via the description of the beloved in the Song of Songs. For a detailed explanation of the imagery and commentaries on some of the poems, see my book *The Gazelle: Medieval Hebrew Poems on God, Israel, and the Soul* (Philadelphia: Jewish Publication Society, 1991), pp. 90–107.

Pp. 320–21

Hermon and Senir: Two names for the same peak in the Anti-Lebanon mountain range, considered to be part of the Land of Israel by the ancients.

Pp. 322–23

Kushan's . . . tents: The biblical phrase (Hab. 3:7) is used here to refer generically to alien lands.

Carmel, Bashan: Mountains in the north of the Land of Israel.

Yokshan, Dishan: Descendants of Abraham (Gen. 25:1–2; 26:20–21) associated, respectively, with the Arabs/Islam, and Rome/Christianity.

Pp. 338–41

A fantastic vision of the angels praising God in the Temple in heaven, a traditional theme of ancient synagogue poetry.